STRANGE DAYS

A SCREENPLAY BY

J B MacCALLUM

FADE IN.

INT. PUB. GLASGOW. NIGHT.(PRESENT DAY)

In a small to average size pub in the Glasgow area we can hear a live band belting out a credible version of a well known pop record from the 1990s and/or contemporary.

The pub is busy with a broad mixture of people doing what people do in pubs. On stage we see a two piece band playing. The singer and lead guitarist, CALLUM 'CAL' RENNIE, 25, accompanied by base guitarist, SEAN GERAGHTY, 25, is clearly in his element singing his heart out.

Cal is a genuinely good singer and the duo clearly have talent but at the end of each number their efforts are rewarded by an audience who are at best mildly entertained and at worst totally indifferent.

Standing at the side of the stage we focus on a woman in her early thirties, ROSIE MARSH, dressed in late nineteenth century clothing and looking older than her years.

ROSIE (V.O.)
(East London)
I've been watching over Callum
Rennie since the day he entered
this world and there's not one
person who knows him better
than me... Nothing remarkable
in that I suppose, except that
in all his twenty five years,
we've never met or said so much
as hello... Then again, ours is
no normal relationship...

INT. MODERN OFFICE. GLASGOW. DAY.

In a sterile modern office environment, we
see that the main working area is divided
into dozens of small cubicles. Each one
containing three to four staff who are busy
on the phone, slavishly bashing away at a
keyboard or absorbed in a PC/VDU screen.

CUBICLE.

Close up of computer screen slowly scrolling
through pages of gobbledegook data. Cal
Rennie is staring at the screen with a
glazed expression. He yawns.

Cal is revealed sitting at a desk in a cubicle. His appearance, although not scruffy, shows the minimum respect for office dress code and his desk/workspace is untidy and cluttered — in contrast to his colleagues.

Cal glances up at a clock on the wall. It is still only 10.10 am. Moments later, GRAHAM CHALMERS, a slim thirty something, full of his own importance, walks in catching Cal by surprise.

> GRAHAM
> (Well spoken Scots)
> How much longer is that going to take you?

> CAL
> (Scots)
> Eh, sorry - What was that?

> GRAHAM
> How much, longer, is that, going, to take you!?

> CAL
> Eh, can't say. The system's running slow this morning.

Graham sighs impatiently.

>   CAL (Cont'd)
>   I am going as fast as
>   I can.

>   GRAHAM
>   Well keep on it. I need
>   it done by first thing
>   tomorrow.

>   CAL
>   First thing! Since when?

>   GRAHAM
>   Since I changed priorities.

>   CAL
>   And how am I supposed to
>   do that!?

>   GRAHAM
>   You'll just have to work
>   late again then won't you.

Although furious Cal manages to suppress
his anger and bite his tongue.

INT. OFFICE. NIGHT.

The office is in darkness except for a small desk lamp and the glow from Cal's computer screen. A desk clock shows 9.40pm. He switches off his workstation, slumps back in his chair and sighs a sigh of relief.

EXT. RESIDENTAL STREET. GLASGOW. NIGHT.

It is late evening and bitterly cold. Outside a typical 1930s sandstone apartment block, an unremarkable hatchback car, at least a decade old, manoeuvres into a parking space.

INT. CAL'S APARTMENT. GLASGOW. NIGHT.

Cal enters the living room of his small apartment, slings a workbag onto the sofa and places his mobile phone on the coffee table. Apart from the period architectural design, the decor is typical of rented accommodation and the furniture fairly old and basic.

In neat rows on the walls hang quality framed pictures of iconic recording artists of the sixties and seventies, including the famous portrait of the Kray twins by David Bailey.

Cal's mobile phone beeps alerting him of a new text. He picks it up and looks at the display. A close up reads.

Hi Cal,
Sorry couldn't be at gig last night,
Needed at work. Hope it went well.
Call you tomorrow.
Kristen XX

Cal switches on the TV then moves to ignite a gas fire set in a wall mounted mantle. As he does, we are drawn to a black and white framed photograph on top of the mantle.

The photo, circa mid 50s, shows a young man in his early 20s with a Elvis style haircut, sitting astride a powerful motorcycle. Standing next to him is a tough looking powerfully built older man and a slightly built youth in his mid teens.

EXT/INT. FACTORY. GLASGOW. NIGHT.(1964)

Standing in a derelict factory, a slim, effeminate looking man, CALVIN RENNIE, 25, with shoulder length bleach blond hair, is waiting looking pensive and worried.

Holding a document folder under one arm, he takes a cigarette out of a packet and lights it with a match. From the way he does this we see he is shaking nervously.

EXT. FACTORY.

An immaculate dark blue Mk 2 Jaguar 3.8 saloon car pulls up outside the factory. Just before the headlights are switched off a close up of the front index plate shows the number FOG 861D.

Two men, BRUCE GEMMELL, 34, a gangland enforcer with the lean chiselled features of a light middleweight boxer, and his younger brother, ARCHIE, 30, get out of the car and walk towards the factory.

INT. FACTORY.

Resume Calvin Rennie. Footsteps approach.

> ARCHIE
> (Glaswegian)
> Evening sugar plum.

> BRUCE
> (To Calvin. Glaswegian)
> You get it?

Trying to avoid eye contact, Calvin nods meekly and hands Bruce the folder.

> CALVIN
> (Effeminate Glaswegian)
> I took it from his case.
> Just like you told me.

Using a small torch, Bruce opens the folder and quickly scans the contents. (At this point we do not see what it is). Archie's eyes light up and he grins greedily.

> CALVIN (Cont'd)
> It's what you wanted
> isn't it?

                    BRUCE
        For your sake it had
        fucking better be.

INT. TAKE-AWAY. GLASGOW. NIGHT. (PRESENT DAY)

Cal walks into an Indian take-away and
approaches the counter. A young Asian man,
INDIJEET, looks pleased to see him.

                    CAL
        Indy... How you doing man?

                    INDIJEET
            (Glaswegian Indian)
        Hey CAL! Sweet man, sweet.
        How's it with you?

                    CAL
        Well it's half ten at night,
        fifty below zero and I've
        just got home from work...
        I think shite just about
        sums it up. If I have to
        spend another day staring
        at a fucking computer my
        brain is going to turn to
        mush.

                    INDIJEET
Jesus, if I had a quid
for every time you said
that... Did you get any
feedback from that record
company?

                     CAL
Yeah, they liked us but
are only interested in
bands with original material.

                    INDIJEET
Still you've got to keep
trying man. You never know
what's around the corner.

                     CAL
That my friend is very true.

EXT. STREET. GLASGOW AREA. DAY.

Wrapped up well to protect himself from the bitter cold, Cal is out jogging in the streets near to where he lives. He runs past a row of individual parking garages. The doors to one garage are open. As he passes he notices a dark blue 1960s MK2 Jaguar saloon car parked within.

Cal stops to look. The car has seen better days. The paint has faded, rust has taken its toll and bits of chrome trim are falling off. The registration plate displays the number FOG 861D.

A MAN in his early sixties approaches.

                    MAN
          Can I help you son?

                    CAL
          Just admiring the car.
          Is it yours?

                    MAN
          Aye.

                    CAL
I love these. They're so
cool. Three point eight?

                    MAN
It is. Seen better days
though.

                    CAL
I've seen worse.

                    MAN
My son and I plan to
restore it.

                    CAL
Good for you.

EXT. STRATHCLYDE LOCH. GLASGOW. DAY.

Cal is jogging through a large area of parkland along a path at the side of a large frozen loch/lake.

In the near distance Cal sees a couple of youngsters on the ice. As he approaches he becomes aware that one of the young boys, BOY 1, is in trouble and appears to have fallen through the ice.

Cal sprints to the scene and discovers his worst fears. One of the boys is struggling desperately about thirty feet out from the bank whilst his friend, Boy 2, looks on helplessly.

                    CAL
        Oh Jesus — no!

                    BOY 2
        MISTER! COME QUICK! My
        brother's fell through
        the ice trying to get
        the dog and he can't
        get out!

With great urgency Cal starts going through the pockets of his fleece jacket and jogging bottoms. His actions becoming more panicked as he realises that he has left his mobile phone at home.

> CAL
> Fuck... How long has
> he been in there!?

> BOY 2
> Five minutes, maybe longer —
> I don't know...

> CAL
> Do you have a phone!?

> BOY 2
> No...

> CAL
> SHIT!... Okay, run. Find
> a phone, find a grown up
> and get them to call 999!...

Cal then spots a couple of people walking with dogs a fair distance away — too far to shout to.

                    CAL (Cont'd)
        Wait — see those two people.
        Get them to call an ambulance
        — go, quick as you can!

Boy two sprints off in the direction of
the dog walkers. Cal then takes his first
tentative steps onto the ice and gingerly
makes his way towards the stricken lad who
is screaming for help.

                    CAL (Cont'd)
        HOLD ON... I'M COMING TO
        GET YOU!

The ice copes with Cal's weight for the first
ten feet or so but after that it begins to
creak and crackle with every step. Further
out Cal is forced to crawl belly down in an
effort to redistribute his mass.

                    CAL (Cont'd)
        Hold on — I'm almost there.

Two feet shy of the boy, Cal senses it too dangerous to inch further. He takes off his fleece jacket and whilst holding on to the sleeve of one arm, tosses the jacket towards the Boy. The first attempt is short but the second lands perfectly within reach.

> CAL (Cont'd)
> Grab the jacket...
> Grab the Jacket!

Although seriously frozen the boy miraculously finds enough strength and dexterity to grab and hold on to the fleece.

> CAL (Cont'd)
> Good lad, now hold on I'm
> going to pull you out!

As Cal takes the strain and starts to haul the boy, the ice crackles become more pronounced and it begins to splinter. Using every ounce of strength he has, Cal pulls the lad inch by inch until he is out of the water and clear of danger.

At the bank, boy 2 arrives with the two dog walkers. One of them, FEMALE DOG WALKER, is talking urgently into a mobile phone, whilst her companion, MALE DOG WALKER, steps on to the ice in a bid to assist.

> MALE DOG WALKER
> The emergency services
> are on their way! Can
> I do anything?

> CAL
> Thank Christ!...
> Yeah, come and take the
> boy!

Without a thought for his own safety, the male dog walker immediately steps onto the ice.

> CAL (Cont'd)
> But for god's sake be
> careful.

Despite being frozen to the bone, boy 1 manages to slowly crawl back towards the bank where he is grabbed by the dog walker and taken to safety.

Meanwhile Cal is just about to retreat when he hears the whimpering yelp of the small terrier dog that is also struggling to escape. Without hesitation he once again tosses his fleece towards the dog in the hope that it will grab it.

> CAL
> Come on doggie, grab it.

The bright little dog grabs the fleece between its teeth and Cal has little trouble hauling the small canine clear of the icy water. Once out the small plucky terrier shakes itself down, barks happily and trots off towards the others.

Back at the ice edge, Cal begins to manoeuvre himself slowly backwards towards the bank. Just as he does there is a sudden loud crack from beneath.

Cal pauses for a moment but when he tries to move again the ice suddenly gives way and he plunges head first into the freezing water. The momentum, shock and the weight of wet clothing, conspire to drag him down.

UNDER WATER.

Under water, Cal manages to halt his descent, re-orients and swims up to the surface. However, such is his haste to escape he is unaware of thick ice directly above him.

Moments later he slams head first into the ice and is knocked cold. With the weight of clothing and no air in his lungs, his body slowly sinks — deeper and deeper into the cold inky blue.

INT. HOSPITAL WARD. GLASGOW. DAY. (1964.)

We open with a scene from sixties TV drama 'Z' Cars. After a few moments the shot pulls back to reveal it shown on a sixties black & white television set.

The shot pulls back further revealing a hospital ward with a dozen or so patients looking enthralled as they watch the unfolding drama... all, except one.

Cal is sitting up in bed looking slightly bewildered. His head is bandaged, his left eye is black and his face is bruised and swollen. A few moments later a NURSE walks to his bed carrying a thermometer.

>   NURSE
>   Open please.

Cal opens his mouth.

>   CAL
>   I realise the NHS is
>   struggling a bit these days
>   but what's going on?

                    NURSE
          What do you mean?

                    CAL
          Well, look at this place,
          you'd think we were back
          in the sixties.

                    NURSE
          You've been unconscious for
          a couple of weeks. You're
          lucky to be alive and that
          nasty bang on the head isn't
          helping matters. Just try to
          relax. All will seem normal
          soon.

The nurse leaves Cal feeling even more
perplexed. She walks towards the end of the
ward, where SISTER MURDOCH is sitting at
her desk.

                    NURSE (Cont'd)
          Better keep an eye on that
          laddie in bed six.
          He's still very confused.

Moments later a smartly dressed thirty year old man, D.C. BAIRD, approaches the Sister's desk and speaks to her. She smiles and points towards Cal. He then walks over.

                    D.C. BAIRD
          Mr Rennie?

                    CAL
          Aye.

                    D.C. BAIRD
          D C Baird. Strathclyde C.I.D.
          How are you feeling today?

                    CAL
          Eh, not bad. A bit sore.

                    D.C. BAIRD
          I'd like to ask a you a few
          questions if that's alright.

                    CAL
          Fair enough.

                    D.C. BAIRD
Apparently you fell from the
Crown Street bridge into the
river at approx one thirty
AM, last Tuesday week... Are
you able to recollect what
happened?

                    CAL
Eh, I think you've been
misinformed officer. Last
thing I remember is falling
through the ice rescuing a
wee boy and his dog.

                    D.C. BAIRD
You fell through ice?

                    CAL
Yes, on Strathclyde Loch.

                    D.C. BAIRD
Mr Rennie, I realise Glasgow
is far from the Tropic of
Cancer, but even the water
here doesn't freeze over in
June.

                    CAL
          June! Christ, how long
          have I been in here?

                D.C. BAIRD
          A little over two weeks.

                    CAL
          Two weeks!? But that can't
          be. It must be almost
          Christmas!

Pause. Carmichael sighs.

                D.C. BAIRD
          According to the doctor, you
          received thirty five stitches
          to a head wound, have three
          broken ribs and extensive
          bruising all over your body.
          Any idea how you came by
          these injuries?

                    CAL
          Not really?

                    D.C. BAIRD
        He also added that apart
        from almost drowning, your
        injuries are typical of
        someone who's just had
        seven shades of shite
        kicked out of them.

                    CAL
        The last thing I remember
        is falling through the ice.

                    D.C. BAIRD
        You're absolutely sure about
        that?

                    CAL
        Absolutely.

D.C. Baird gets up from the chair as if to
leave. As he does he momentarily ponders
one last question.

                    D.C. BAIRD
        I don't suppose the name
        Bruce Gemmell means anything
        to you?

                        CAL
            Can't say it does.

                     D.C. BAIRD
            Thanks for your time Mr
            Rennie. We'll talk again.

D.C. Baird walks towards the exit. As he
does he passes the Sister's desk. He smiles
to her and says 'Cheerio'. She responds
likewise - just as her desk phone rings.

                   SISTER MURDOCH
            Hello, Livingston ward...

INT. PHONE BOX. GLASGOW. DAY. (1964)

In a public telephone box a man in his mid twenties, BOBBY GEMMELL, is talking into the handset.

>   BOBBY
>   (Glaswegian)
>   Can you tell me if you have
>   a patient there called Calvin
>   Rennie please?
>   (Few beats)
>   I'm his cousin and I was just
>   wondering how he is?
>   (Few beats)
>   I see, aye... aye... Oh is
>   he, that's good news.
>   (Few beats)
>   His memory — Oh dear that's
>   a shame… We'll just have to
>   hope and pray then……

INT. JAGUAR CAR. GLASGOW. DAY. (1964)

Bobby gets into the back of Bruce's Jag and shuts the door. Sitting in it are Bruce and Archie Gemmell.

> BOBBY
> He's alive.

> ARCHIE
> What!? Aw, I don't fucking believe it!

Bruce's disappointment smoulders.

INT. HOSPITAL WARD. GLASGOW. NIGHT. (1964)

Cal, clearly in pain, is limping along the ward. He enters a door with the sign, Male Toilet/Bathroom.

TOILET/BATHROOM

We see Cal flushing the toilet. He then moves to the sink to wash his hands. Whilst doing so he looks at himself curiously in the mirror. Something isn't quite right.

Although he has a bandage wrapped around his forehead, and his face is cut, swollen and covered in bruising, it's the tuft of bleach blond hair that really takes his notice.

He partially unwraps the head bandage — which to his great astonishment reveals bleach blond, shoulder length hair.

                    CAL
          What the fuck?!

Then, behind him, reflected in the mirror, Rosie Marsh suddenly appears startling the life out of him. She breathes in and grimaces

                    ROSIE
          Agh, Jeez-us...

Startled, Cal turns to face her.

                    CAL
          Do you mind!

                    ROSIE
              (Fanning her nose)
         No kidding... If you don't
         get that window open pretty
         damn pronto, even the rats
         will be heaving.

                    CAL
         What?!

Observing Rosie's Victorian clothing, Cal
looks bewildered.

                    ROSIE
         Seriously Callum.

Before Cal has a chance to react, the bottom
frame of the sash window suddenly lifts and
shoots open of its own accord. Rosie then
moves to it and takes several deep breaths
of fresh air.

                    CAL
              (Bewildered)
         W-who a-are you?...

                    ROSIE
          I'm Rosie...
          Your guardian angel...
               (Beat)
          Nice to meet you at last.

Cal is rendered momentarily speechless.

                    CAL
          Is this some sort of wind
          up?

                    ROSIE
          Why does everyone always say
          that... How about, Hi Rosie,
          nice to meet you too... And
          why in the name of sweet
          Jesus, do I look like a cross
          between Boris Karloff and
          Jimmy Savile.

Cal looks back in the mirror at himself.

                    CAL
          What the fuck's going on?

                    ROSIE
              (After beat)
In nineteen sixty four,
a young man, same age as
yourself, died in the river
below the Crown St bridge.
His name was Calvin Rennie...
              (Beat)
However, according to destiny
he was supposed to die of a
stroke two weeks ago, aged
eighty three... Which by
complete coincidence just
happened to be exactly the same
date and time that you fell
into the loch and drowned.

                    CAL
I drowned?

                    ROSIE
Yes, and no. Destiny was
expecting the other 'Cal'
Rennie but because of some
admin balls up they got
your soul instead... which
is a problem cos you aren't
scheduled to die for quite
some time yet.

CAL

How the fuck can they mix
us up? My name's Callum not
Calvin.

ROSIE

A glitch in the new computer
system. Gabriel may be the
first angel of the moon but
when it comes to software
he's a total arse.

CAL

So if I'm not scheduled to
die yet, what am I doing in
this place? Why don't I look
like me anymore?

INT. JAGUAR CAR. DAY. (1964)

The Gemmell Brothers are driving through Glasgow in Bruce's Jag. Archie is driving.

> BRUCE
> I give you one, easy, simple task and you still manage to fuck it up!... I might as well given the job to Pinky and fucking Perky!

> ARCHIE
> He was half dead when we threw him in! How many more times!

> BOBBY
> A good kicking you said. Nothing about killing the poor bastard!

> BRUCE
> Oh, poor bastard is it now... Would this happen to be the same poor bastard who just cost us fifteen grand! He fucked up, he knows too much. End of!

BOBBY

But you're talking about
murder.

BRUCE

And I suppose you'd rather
he blabbed everything to
the fucking police?

BOBBY

But he's just as guilty as
we are. He's scared shitless.

BRUCE

All the more reason. It's
what's known in the trade
as covering your arse.

BOBBY

He went twenty minutes without
oxygen. The hospital said he's
confused and can't remember
anything. Who he is, fuck
all... If you ask me there's a
good chance he's brain damaged.

BRUCE

He'll get on alright with
you two then.

INT. BATHROOM. HOSPITAL. NIGHT. (1964)

Resume Cal and Rosie.

>   CAL
>   So let me get this right.
>   Because of this mix up
>   between me and this Calvin
>   fella, destiny has put
>   my soul into a state of
>   spiritual limbo?

>   ROSIE
>   That's right.

>   CAL
>   And to try to solve this
>   problem you have transferred
>   my soul into the dead body
>   of Calvin Rennie who last
>   drew breath in nineteen
>   sixty four?

>   ROSIE
>   It's only temporary.

>   CAL
>   And how long's that for?

                ROSIE
No idea.

                CAL
No idea? How I am supposed
to survive in someone else's
body in a fifty eight year old
parallel dimension?

                ROSIE
You've always wanted to
experience the swinging
sixties.

                CAL
But what am I going to do
for money?

                ROSIE
Calvin's got money.
Everything that's his is
now yours.

INT. WARD. HOSPITAL. DAY. (1964)

Cal is sitting on the side of the bed, when a nurse walks up carrying a pile of clothes. She places them on the bed.

> NURSE
> Your clothes Mr Rennie.

It's the flowery orangey satin shirt with the huge droopy collars that catches his eye. Then the bright red trousers and black leather waistcoat. Cal unfolds the shirt with a look of distain.

LATER. SISTER'S DESK.

Cal is standing by the Sister's desk, fully clothed looking very uncomfortable and feeling pretty ridiculous.

> CAL
> I don't suppose I had a coat?

> SISTER MURDOCK
> I'm afraid not.

From her desk drawer Sister Murdock produces an envelope and empties the contents on to her desk. A wallet, a cigarette lighter, a few coins, a key ring and a library card.

Callum picks up the wallet and opens it. In it is few pound notes. Sister Murdock shows him a patient inventory and offers him a pen.

> SISTER MURDOCK (Cont'd)
> Are you sure I can't persuade
> you to reconsider Mr Rennie?

> CAL
> I'll be fine thank you.

> SISTER MURDOCK
> Very well then but the
> second you feel any stomach
> pains, nausea, dizziness or
> continued memory loss, get
> yourself back to us as soon
> as possible.

EXT. HOSPITAL. GLASGOW. DAY. (1964)

Cal walks out of the hospital and into the
surrounding streets. He is immediately hit
by the look and smell of a city fifty eight
years in the past. On paper it doesn't seem
so long ago but in reality it is.

As he walks along the street Cal's feelings
of self conscious intensify as everyone he
passes, especially men, seem to glance at
him with distain or derision.

Further down the street we become aware of
a large Humber saloon car following close
behind. The car moves closer until it is
right beside him - driven at walking pace.

The driver's door window winds down, allowing
us to see the driver. ANDREW WISHART, is a
slim, dapper looking gentleman in his early
fifties, with whitish grey hair.

                    WISHART
               (Cultured Scots)
            Calvin... Calvin!...

Cal looks round. The car stops.

                    WISHART (Cont'd)
        They told me you were
        getting out. Thank god
        you are alright.

Wishart expects a reaction but Cal doesn't
let on.

                    WISHART (Cont'd)
        I have been out of my mind
        with worry. If anything had
        happened to you I would have
        died myself.

                    CAL
        Sorry, do I know you?

                    WISHART
        Look you have every right
        to be miffed. I wanted
        nothing more than to come
        and see you but visiting
        was simply impossible.

                    CAL
        You still haven't answered
        my question?

                    WISHART
      What's that?

                     CAL
      Who are you?

                    WISHART
      Look why don't you just get
      in and we can go somewhere
      less conspicuous.

                     CAL
      Don't take this the wrong
      way pal but I'm not in the
      habit of getting into cars
      with strange men... know
      what I mean..

Callum walks away leaving Wishart looking
rather confused.

                    WISHART
      Oh my god, how thoughtless.
      Forgive me, I am so sorry.
      Please let me give you a
      lift home. After all,
      I am your Uncle.

                    CAL
        Uncle! Christ man why
        didn't you say so?

INT. WISHARTS CAR. DAY. (1964)

                    WISHART
        You sound different?

                    CAL
        I've picked up a throat
        infection from the water.
        All the chemicals and shit.

                    WISHART
        You seem different too?

                    CAL
        Maybe I'll feel more like my
        old self when I get out of
        these stupid clothes. I feel
        a right wanker.

                    WISHART
        I thought you loved that
        shirt?

                    CAL
You're joking. What sort of
numptie would buy a shirt
like this.

                  WISHART
Eh, I did... On our last
weekend away together.

                    CAL
Weekend away together?

                  WISHART
In Bruges — remember?...
And a beautiful gold neck
chain to go with it.

                    CAL
        (After momentary ponder)
Pull over.

                  WISHART
Pardon?

                    CAL
I said pull over!

                  WISHART
Why, what's the matter?

                    CAL
        PULL THE FUCKING CAR OVER…
        NOW!!

Taken aback, Wishart pulls the car over and
stops.

                    WISHART
        Calvin, whatever's wrong!?

                    CAL
        My uncle are you?
        I bloody bet you are!

Cal opens the car door and quickly gets
out.

                    CAL (Cont'd)
        Listen pal, whatever went
        on between us is over,
        right!… Done for! No
        longer interested.
        So fuck off don't bother
        me again!.

Cal slams the car door shut and walks off,
leaving Wishart totally gobsmacked.

EXT. CAMPBELL STREET. GLASGOW. DAY. (1964)

It is early evening. Campbell Street is dominated by grey, grimy three storey tenement buildings. Callum takes a library card from his pocket. A close up reveals a name and address. Calvin Iain Rennie. 23 Campbell Street, Drumchapel.

INT. TENEMENT FLAT. LIVING ROOM. DAY. (1964)

Cal opens the living room door and switches on the light illuminating a sparsely furnished living room. The flooring is a sepia coloured linoleum, partially covered by a large Paisley rug and in the corner stands a old TV.

On top of the fireplace mantle is a framed photo. It is a picture of Calvin Rennie posing beside a street sign marked 'CARNABY STREET'

BEDROOM.

In the bedroom Callum opens a tallboy drawer revealing underwear and socks. From the drawer below he pulls out a couple of tee shirts and a roll neck sweater.

In a wardrobe, among a selection of loud shirts and colourful trousers, he finds a pair of jeans and a small holdall. He places both items on the bed then opens the holdall to see what's inside.

There is nothing of any great interest, but buried at the bottom of the holdall Cal finds a small tin tea box. He looks inside and is pleasantly surprised to discover £75 in bank notes (Today approx £1,600) and a gold neck chain.

LATER. BATHROOM.

In the bathroom, dressed only in a pair of 'y' fronts, Cal looks at himself in a wall mirror. (His rib area is still badly bruised) Then, with a large pair of scissors, he zealously starts cutting off his long dyed blond hair.

(As he does this we see a distinctive semi circular jagged shaped scar on the right hand side of his upper chest.)

EXT. STREET. TENEMENT BLOCK. NIGHT.(1964)

The Gemmell brothers Jaguar saloon car enters Campbell Street and stops opposite the tenement block. The brothers look up at Calvin Rennie's flat. The lights are on.

                    BRUCE
          Brain damage my arse.

INT. TENEMENT FLAT. NIGHT. (1964)

Callum, now sporting a short rough haircut, exits the bedroom dressed in a thick roll neck jumper and jeans. He is carrying the holdall he found in the wardrobe and puts it down on the floor next to the front door. Just as he does there is a knock at the front door..

After a brief pause he cautiously opens it just wide enough to see who is there... Then WALLOP! It suddenly bursts open, hitting him full in the face, causing him to reel backwards.

As Cal stands dazed and barely able to stand, the Gemmell bros barge into the flat and surround him.

> BRUCE
> Well, well, if it's not
> the queer from Atlantis...

Archie laughs. Bobby is more restrained. Cal groans holding his hand over a bleeding nose.

                    BRUCE (Cont'd)
          Or to be more accurate, the
          totally fucking useless queer
          from Atlantis!

                    CAL
          Who are you!?... What do you
          want!?

The Gemmell's look at one another with
puzzled amusement. (considering Cal looks
genuinely bewildered) Bruce takes out a
Browning pistol and cocks it.

                    BRUCE
          Dreams, ambitions, escape
          to a better life... Things
          that aren't going to happen
          because you fucked up!..
          FIFTEEN FUCKING GRANDS WORTH!

                    CAL
          Fifteen grand!..
          What are you on about!?

                    ARCHIE
          Can you believe this prick...

                    CAL
      I don't know what you're on
      about, honest to god I don't!

                    BOBBY
      There's something no right
      here.

Bruce aims the pistol at one of Cal's knees
and puts pressure on the trigger.

                    BRUCE
Perhaps this will jog your memory...

                    CAL
      NO, NO WAIT! I can explain!..
      You think I'm Calvin right?
      But I'm not. I'm eh...
      Ronnie, Calvin's brother,
      we're identical twins!

Bruce pauses for a moment. The bros glance
at one another.

                    BRUCE
      Ronnie Rennie?

                    CAL
          Yeah Ronnie - I've just come
          up to visit from, eh, London.

                    BOBBY
          This can't be Calvin. Look at
          him. He's totally different.
          His mannerisms, voice,
          everything.

Bruce and Archie ponder the situation.

                    ARCHIE
          He does seem very different.
          Fuck it - shoot him anyway.

                    BRUCE
          So where did the cuts and
          bruises come from?

                    CAL
          I was mugged.

                    BRUCE
          So where is he?

>   CAL
>   Calvin, eh, still in
>   hospital.

>   BRUCE
>   He was discharged this
>   morning!

Losing patience, Bruce grabs Cal around the throat and pushes the pistol into his face

>   BRUCE (Cont'd)
>   SO WHERE THE FUCK IS HE!?

>   CAL
>   I don't know —
>   at my folks maybe.

>   BRUCE
>   Archie check the rooms.

Archie exits towards the other rooms. Bruce, still holding Callum around the throat, forces him backwards into the kitchenette.

BEDROOM.

Archie enters the main bedroom and looks around. After a quick check of the wardrobe he notices Cal's discarded clothes lying on top of the bed.

BATHROOM.

Archie then enters the bathroom and switches on the light. Something low down immediately catches his eye. He smirks.

KITCHENETTE.

The kitchenette is small with the sink and window at the far end. Cal is standing with his back to the sink, trapped between it and the only exit which is covered by Bruce and his brother Bobby. Archie returns looking pleased with himself.

                    ARCHIE
          Look what I found.

In one hand Archie holds up the flowery shirt. In the other he reveals several long cuttings of dyed blond hair. Bruce grabs one and looks at it.

                    CAL
     I cut my hair so what.

                    ARCHIE
     Go Brucie, do the wee fucker!
     DO HIM!

                    BRUCE
     You piece of shit!

                    CAL
     Jesus man! NO WAIT!!
     You can't shoot me you'll
     fuck everything up!

As Bruce's finger squeezes on the trigger
Bobby turns the other way. Cal can only
look on helplessly... Then.

                    ARCHIE
       HOLD IT! HOLD IT!...
       Can I do it?...
       I've haven't shot anyone
       for ages.

Bruce reluctantly hands the gun to a
delighted Archie.

                    BRUCE
          No pissing about. Two in the
          head. Two in the chest.

                    ARCHIE
          Can I put one in his balls
          first?

                    BRUCE
          No!

Archie beams broadly as he takes aim at Cal.
He squeezes the trigger... Then CRACK!! The
pistol discharges...

Cal grimaces, bracing himself for the impact
of the bullet.

However, from a couple of feet away Archie
has managed to miss and put a round through
a tin bread bin, causing the bullet to
ricochet through the kitchen window.

                    BRUCE
          In the name of Christ! How
          the fuck did you manage
          that!?

                    ARCHIE
        I don't know. My arm just
        sort of moved.

                    BRUCE
        What do you mean it moved!?
        He's two fucking feet away
        you squint eyed cunt!

                    ARCHIE
        It did, like somebody
        pushed it!

Then to Cal's great surprise and relief,
Rosie Marsh manifests right next to Archie
- unseen to the brothers.

                    ROSIE
                (To Cal)
        I dunno, I leave you alone
        for five bloody minutes...

                    CAL
        ROSIE! Thank Christ!

Unable to see Rosie, the Gemmell's are
momentarily distracted and slightly
dumbfounded.

CAL (Cont'd)
They're going to shoot me!

ROSIE
You don't say... Now when
I say run, you go like
Usain Bolt with a hot
poker up his arse.

BRUCE
(To Archie)
Now stop pissing about and
get on with it!

Once again Archie takes careful aim, unaware
that Rosie is standing beside him. Then,
with perfect timing, at the split second he
pulls the trigger, she yanks his arm down
90 degrees causing him to shoot his own
foot.

ROSIE
RUN!!

Gifted with the chance to escape, Cal
launches himself rugby style at a
screaming Archie, knocking him over into
his brothers.

As Archie hits the floor his pistol discharges twice - the first bullet passing so close to Bruce's head it takes the top off his left ear, the second demolishing the living room light - plunging the room into darkness.

With Archie on the floor writhing in agony, Bruce temporarily stunned and Bobby on his backside, Callum manages to force his way past and dash through the dimly lit room towards the front door. Just as he goes to open it.

> ROSIE (Cont'd)
> (Pointing to holdall)
> CAL!... Bag!

Cal quickly turns, grabs hold of the holdall and exits the flat as fast as he can.

> BRUCE
> THE BASTARD'S GETTING AWAY!!

With blood streaming down the side of his face and the top of his ear hanging off, Bruce snatches the pistol from Archie and charges after Cal.

Just as Bruce runs past, Rosie sticks out her leg sending him crashing to the floor. However, Bruce quickly springs back onto his feet, wrenches open the door and storms out.

INTERCUT — STAIRWELL/COURTYARD.

Callum scrambles down the stairwell towards the exit with Bruce in angry pursuit.

Callum exits the block into the courtyard as fast as he can. As Bruce bursts out of the block, he sees Cal running ahead about fifty yards and immediately fires four well aimed rounds at him. Cal, head held low, runs past a couple parked cars to shield himself as bullets puncture bodywork and shatter windows.

Like a man possessed Bruce continues the chase. His pace quicker, fitter and more committed than Cal who is beginning to flag.

Callum makes it to a corner just as two more rounds slam into brickwork dangerously close. He turns the corner and immediately crashes into some dustbins and falls. Quickly scrambling back on to his feet he spots a dimly lit alleyway.

As Bruce reaches the same corner Cal is nowhere to be seen. Bruce desperately listens for the sound of someone running.

But now, with the sound of approaching police sirens, Bruce has no choice but to withdraw. Seething with anger he turns and walks back towards the tenement.

EXT. STREET/URBAN AREA. GLASGOW. NIGHT. (1964)

Callum is running through the streets. He looks pretty exhausted. His breathing and stride appear laboured and he is clutching his side. (ribs)

Further along, gasping for breath and satisfied that all is clear, he slithers down a wall onto his backside - his relief plain to see. Moments later, Rosie manifests.

                    ROSIE
          That was a close one.

                    CAL
              (Still gasping)
What the fuck's going on?
They said I lost them fifteen
grand, that's over four
hundred thousand in today's
money! What sort of shit have
you landed me in?

                   ROSIE
Alright, I admit that the
situation you find yourself
in is far from ideal but...

                    CAL
They were going to shoot me
for fuck sake!

                   ROSIE
Calvin's life is a bit
complicated.

                    CAL
A bit complicated!? Fuck
that. You put me in this
situation, now you get me
out of it!

ROSIE

Cal this isn't Randal and
Hopkirk... I can't just can't
yank you out, things have
been set in motion. The only
thing I can do, from now on,
is give you guidance...
       (Beat)
I'm sorry but if you want
your soul back you're just
going to have to grow a pair
and get on with it.

EXT. CENTRAL LONDON. DAY. (1964)

We see Callum strolling through town experiencing the heart and soul of mid sixties swinging London. He is now clean shaven, his hair is short and tidy and he is dressed head to toe in a new set of contemporary sixties clothes.

SERIES OF SHOTS A. LONDON. DAY. (1964)

A1. INT. HIGH TECH OFFICE. DAY.

A smartly dressed Cal enters an office and approaches the reception.

> CAL
> Callum Rennie. I have an interview at ten thirty.

COMPUTER ROOM.

A white coated BOFFIN type leads Cal towards a door marked 'Computer Room — Authorised Personnel Only'.

> BOFFIN
>
> Not only is she one of the most advanced, she's also one of the smallest.

As they enter the computer room the sight of the computer makes Callum's jaw drop. It almost fills the entire room.

A2. INT. CLERICAL OFFICE. DAY:

An unhappy looking Cal is sitting at a desk sifting through a huge pile of paper forms, monotonously stamping each one, whilst enveloped in a thick cloud of cigarette smoke, exhaled from a dozen chain smoking colleagues.

EXT. HIGH STREET. EAST LONDON. DAY. (1964)

It is early morning and lashing with rain. A dejected looking Callum is riding a Post Office issue bicycle along a busy street, wearing a Post Office issue waterproof.

He comes to a small music shop and is immediately enthralled by the variety of instruments in the front window display. As he is putting the mail through the letter box, he notices a printed A4 flyer taped onto the door glass.

NEW TALENT SHOWCASE!... See the chart stars of tomorrow TODAY! Live at the Hope & Anchor. Saturday 16th Oct.

INT. ROUGH PUB. GLASGOW. EVENING. (1964)

In a grim looking pub called the 'Auld Shank', where hard looking men are served from behind iron bars, Archie Gemmell (with bandaged foot) is talking to two young women, SHEENA & JANIS.

>   ARCHIE
>   So I says to this bastard,
>   you've got ten seconds to
>   hand me the cash before I
>   slice off your balls and shove
>   them down your throat...
>   Next thing I know he's pulled
>   a nine mill out of nowhere
>   and shoved it in my face!...
>   Fuck you he says!... I tried
>   to take the gun off him but
>   the fucking thing went off and
>   took two of my toes with it.

Bruce Gemmell walks into the pub and approaches the bar. Tough looking men respectfully move out of his way and others greet him. His demeanour however, isn't moody or menacing. He spots Archie and beckons him over.

                    ARCHIE (Cont'd)
          Back in a sec.

Archie gets up on crutches and hobbles over
to his brother.

                    SHEENA
          He's so full of shite
          he aught to be drinking
          Domestos.

Janis agrees. At the bar, the BARMAID greets
Bruce and asks him what he wants.

                    BRUCE
          Double Morangie please hen.
                (Then to Archie)
          Our problem just got worse.

Bruce hands Archie a newspaper and points
to a headline and accompanying photograph.
A close up of the front page shows a sub-
headline. It reads... *'MINISTER SUSPENDED
IN RENT BOY SCANDAL!'*

A close up of photograph shows Andrew
Wishart, standing outside a government
building, full of pompous defiance.

ARCHIE

Shit!... Wishart...!

BRUCE

We better prey they find out
nothing about him and Rennie.
Because if they do we are
well and truly fucked...

EXT. PUB VENUE. NORTH LONDON. EVENING (1964)

We see a close up of a billposter. *'Tonight
at the Hope & Anchor — NEW BAND SHOWCASE.*

INT. PUB VENUE. NORTH LONDON. EVENING (1964)

With a his guitar case slung over his back, Cal is standing at the bar waiting to be served in a large Victorian pub. On stage, a very average four-piece R&B band are belting out a pop song of the period.

In a large mirror behind the bar he catches the reflection of a very attractive brunette. HANNAH JENSEN, is 25, slim with blue eyes and shoulder length hair - and Cal can't take his eyes off her. She is next in line to be served but for some strange reason the barman moves to serve him.

                    CAL
          I believe this lovely lady
          was next.

The barman nods and serves Hannah.

                    HANNAH
          Thank you.

As Hannah gives the barman her order, Cal can't help scanning the pert sexy bum that fills her jeans so perfectly, her long shapely legs and tight black roll neck that contours her equally impressive torso.

                    HANNAH (Cont'd)
          Are you playing tonight?

                    CAL
          Thought I'd give it a go.

                    HANNAH
          Good for you...
          I'll look out for you.

                    CAL
          Just as long as you don't
          shower me with rotten
          vegetables.

                    HANNAH
                 (Laughs)
          I can't make any promises.

Hannah picks up the drinks and makes her way back to her friends. Callum can't help watching her as she walks away. The flirtatious encounter, brief as it was, has generated a warm glow in his cheeks and put a twinkle back in his eyes.

                    BARMAN
          Yes mate?

                     CAL
          Pint of bitter please.

As the barman proceeds with the order, Cal's eyes follow Hannah to a table where she joins a group of friends. (Mostly men holding guitars) Then, from behind him.

                    ROSIE
          I bet she doesn't go out
          with postmen.

Cal turns expecting to see Rosie but she is nowhere to be seen. Then a girl, sitting on a bar stool with her back to him, turns round. To his great surprise it is Rosie, dressed in fashionable sixties clothes, hair, makeup, etc.

                    CAL
Rosie! Wow! I don't believe it.
What's with the clothes? I would
never have recognised you.

                   ROSIE
I'm fed up looking like Mary
Poppins. Nineteenth century
underwear is so rough you
might as well be dragged down
the street on your bare arse.

                    CAL
Well I must say it really
suits you.

                   ROSIE
Thank you kindly young man.

                    CAL
So where have you been?
Haven't seen you in weeks?

                   ROSIE
I've been around. Still been
keeping an eye.

                    CAL
I thought you'd abandoned me.

                    ROSIE
Nah.. Just thought I'd give
you a bit of space that's
all. You don't seem to be
doing too bad.

                    CAL
I'm a postman.

                    ROSIE
Nothing doing in computers
then?

                    CAL
Please. Computer technology's
still in the dark ages. Last
job I went for the mainframe
was bigger than St Paul's.

                    ROSIE
Still, at least you don't
look like a pantomime poofter
no more.
        (Beat)
In actual fact you look
uncannily like, well eh, you.

                    CAL
You never know. Perhaps me
and Calvin are related.

                   ROSIE
        (After beat)
Anyway, what do you make of
swinging London then?

                    CAL
My head's buzzing. It's my
every dream and nightmare
rolled into one. It's totally
surreal. Everything's
familiar, yet so different -
if that makes sense.

                   ROSIE
Tell me about it. I remember
this place when it first
opened.

                    CAL
Wow. When was that?

                   ROSIE
Eighteen eighty eight. The
year I snuffed it. I was
thirty three.

                    ROSIE (Cont'd)
         Thirty three years of shit.
         I've had a much better life
         dead than I ever did alive...

                    CAL
         How come?

                    ROSIE
         Well for starters I don't
         have to give thr'penny
         blowjobs in cold dark
         alleys no more.

ON STAGE.

A COMPÈRE introduces the next act.

                    COMPÈRE
         Put your hands together
         for the totally groovy...
         BARRACUDAS!!

Applause etc. The Barracuda's are a four
piece R&B band lead by vocalist, KRYS
WINSLOW. The other members are JEFF GRUNDY
(Lead guitar/vocals/keyboard), VIC EASTER
(Bass guitar) and TERRY 'WAG' GILHOOLY
(Drums)

Standing in the audience is, OLLIE JACKSON, a cross between Austin Powers and Humpty Dumpty, sporting a mop hairstyle and black-rimmed Harry Palmer style glasses.

                    KRYS
          A... ONE, TWO, THREE, FOUR!!

The Barracuda's intro is strong. The tightness, rhythm and quality of their musicianship immediately commands attention — that is until Winslow opens his mouth.

It isn't that his voice is terribly bad, it's just that it isn't terribly good either. The lyrics are hackneyed and the melody doesn't really flow. (Chorus below)

Groovy chick, so sexy and neat
kind'a girl that I wanna meet,
Groovy chick I wanna know what
you're know-in
Groovy chick I wanna go where
you're go-in
Think of you baby all of the
time... coz
Groovy chick, you're blow-in my
mind, Yeh! yeh!

Krys however, does have one ace up his sleeve — his tall dark good looks and his dynamic, albeit, affected stage presence.

> ROSIE
> Singer's a bit of wanker.

> CAL
> Shame, the band's really good.

LATER.

When The Barracuda's finish the reaction from the audience is pretty positive. Krys leaps from the stage, goes to Hannah, the girl Cal met at the bar, and gives her a big hug.

> ROSIE
> You're on mate... Good luck.

Guitar in hand, Callum walks onto the stage. The compère introduces him.

> COMPÈRE
> Okay, we have a solo act for you now. All the way from Bonnie Scotland... please welcome JACK DALLAS!

The audience applauds. Callum (AKA Jack Dallas) takes a few moments to make himself comfortable, then just as he is about to hit the first chord.

KRYS WINSLOW
DONALD WHERE'S MA TROOZERS!!

Krys thinks he's a right wag. A few members of the audience laugh but not as many as he would have hoped. A close up of Ollie shows him giving Krys a contemptuous look — a feeling shared by Hannah and the rest of the Band.

Note: The song Cal performs is one that has been written within the last 25 years, is complemented by an acoustic guitar and wouldn't seem out of place in the mid sixties. The quality of Cal's guitar playing hooks the audience instantly. As does the song and his voice. A shot of Krys Winslow, shows the smile well and truly wiped off his face.

HANNAH
Wow, this guy's pretty good.

OLLIE
(West country)
He's is indeed.

LATER.

When Cal finishes he is warmly cheered and applauded. He loves it.

> CAL
> WOW... That felt great!

> ROSIE
> Jack Dallas. Very rock and roll.

Moments later, Cal is approached by Ollie Jackson.

> OLLIE
> Jack Dallas?... Hi, name's Ollie Jackson.

> CAL
> Pleased to meet you.

> OLLIE
> Got to tell you man, I thought you were far out. Vibrant, original. I really think you have something.

> CAL
> Really - thanks very much.

                    OLLIE
          Do you have more material
          like that?

INT. MUSIC SHOP. LONDON. DAY (1964)

Ollie is showing Callum around a large
music shop that sells a wide variety of
musical instruments and records. Cal is
particularly captivated by the impressive
array of guitars.

                    OLLIE
          But the most interesting part
          of my business is in the
          basement.

BASEMENT RECORDING STUDIO.

Through a door (with STUDIO on it) Ollie
leads Cal into a small, but well equipped,
recording studio. Relaxing and jamming
there are the members of The Barracudas,
accompanied by the lovely Hannah. Ollie
introduces Cal to everyone.

Each of them greets in a warm and friendly manner — with the exception of Krys, who remains aloof and only manages a reluctant "Hi". (He is wearing shades in a basement.)

                    CAL
               (To Hannah)
          We meet again.

                    HANNAH
          We do indeed. I've even got
          the rotten veggies ready.
          But if the other night was
          anything to go by, I don't
          think I'll be needing them.

Close up of Krys's reaction. Cal & Hannah hold their gaze a little too long for his liking.

                    KRYS
          I hear you've got some tunes?

                    CAL
          A few.

                    KRYS
          Then what are you waiting
          for. Knock us out man.

With the others listening expectantly,
Cal settles himself and hits them with an
acoustic version of?

Again, contemporary-ish tracks that could be
comfortably adapted into a sixties context.
EG: Amy Winehouse, Duffy, Adele, Oasis, Paul
Weller, etc. Cal does two or three songs.
Up-tempo and ballad.

By the time Callum has finished his set
he has generated genuine excitement. Krys
however, remains muted.

> JEFF
> (Mancunian)
> Wow man — you got any more
> stuff like that!?

> CAL
> Loads.

> TERRY
> And you write everything
> yourself?

Callum hesitates momentarily as a beaming
Hannah catches his eye.

                    CAL
        Everything.

More ad-lib praise etc. Hannah looks
especially impressed. Ollie notices Krys's
reticence.

                    KRYS
        Ollie... A word man.

CORRIDOR. OUTSIDE STUDIO.

                    KRYS
        What the fuck is Jock strap
        doing here!?

                    OLLIE
        I invited him.

                    KRYS
        Oh, I see. And you just sort
        of did so without telling me?

                    OLLIE
        I did. The other night at
        Sophie's party.

                    KRYS
        I don't remember.

                    OLLIE

When do you ever remember?

                    KRYS

Okay, okay. But it still
doesn't explain why he's
here?

                    OLLIE

I want him in the band.

                    KRYS

What? You're joking.

                    OLLIE

I've never been more serious.

                    KRYS

No way man... No fucking way!

                    OLLIE

Jack has got the two vital
ingredients that we need...
Inspiration and originality.

                    KRYS

So he's written a few half
decent tunes. What's wrong
with my stuff?

OLLIE

Nothing! Nothing wrong at
all, if you want to spend
the rest of your days playing
pubs, clubs and Sally army
halls.

KRYS

So what are you saying!?

OLLIE

I'm saying the Barracudas are
just another good R&B band
going nowhere. Jack Dallas
can change all that and
that's an opportunity
way too good to miss!
     (Beat)
And if you don't like it,
tough shit.

EXT. CLUB VENUE. LONDON. NIGHT. (1964)

A close up of a bill poster reads *'THE PURPLE PUSSY PRESENTS'... THE BEATROOTS – THE GILES MILES BIG SOUND — LONE WOOLFE — THE BARRACUDAS.*

STAGE.

On stage at a small club venue, we see Cal and The Barracudas in action, belting out their version of ******?

> ROSIE (V.O.)
> In a short while, thanks
> to the addition of Cal and
> a couple of dozen ripped off
> tunes, The Barracudas found
> a brand new lease of life.

Standing at the side of the stage, next to Ollie, Hannah catches Cal's eye. She smiles and gives him a little wave.

> ROSIE (V.O. Cont'd)
> And Cal loved every minute.

INT. PUB/BAR. GLASGOW. NIGHT. (1964)

Scene opens with a NEWSCASTER reading the
BBC evening news on a black and white TV.

> NEWSCASTER
> Andrew Wishart, the disgraced
> former defence minister, was
> jailed for two years at the
> high court today.

TV cuts to a shot of a humiliated Wishart,
being led in handcuffs and put into the back
of a prison van.

> NEWSCASTER (Cont'd)
> The fifty three year old
> bachelor, who was forced to
> resign following allegations
> of employing the services of
> rent boys, was found guilty
> of perverting the course of
> justice after it was proved
> he lied under oath.

Shot pulls out to reveal Bruce, Archie and
Bobby Gemmell leaning against a snooker
table, watching the TV report.

                    ARCHIE
         Fucking old queer.

                    BOBBY
         At least he kept his
         trap shut.

                    BRUCE
              (After beat)
         For now anyway...

INT. PHARMACY. LONDON. DAY. (1964)

A PHARMACIST hands Callum a box of sleeping
pills.

                    PHARMACIST
         Insomnadol. Take one of
         these half an hour before
         bed and I guarantee you'll
         be out for hours.

                    CAL
         Ok thanks.

EXT. HIGH STREET. LONDON AREA. DAY. (1964)

As Cal walks past a newspaper vendor his eyes are drawn to a headline and he is immediately taken aback. It reads: *RENT BOY MINISTER JAILED*. An editorial photo shows Wishart being led from court in handcuffs.

SERIES OF SHOTS B.

B1. INT. MIXING STUDIO.

The band relax, with drinks in hand, as Ollie and an ENGINEER play back the demo tape. They all look pretty pleased with themselves.

> ROSIE (V.O.)
> Over the next couple of
> months things seemed to be
> well and truly on the up. The
> gigs were sell outs and Ollie
> had put his money where his
> mouth is.

B2. INT. OLLIE'S OFFICE.

Ollie talking on the phone. (Note: Hanging on wall behind Ollie's desk is a framed photo of him posing with a Barracuda fish he has caught)

B3. OFFICE. MUSICAL AGENTS.

Sitting behind a large desk, in an office covered in posters and photos of well known sixties pop stars, MAX, a portly, self important, cigar puffing man, is listening to the Barracudas demo tape with Ollie. He nods his approval.

> ROSIE (V.O. Cont'd)
> True to his word, he worked his arse off, meeting with, bribing and pleading with as many people as he could.

B4. INT. OLLIE'S OFFICE. LONDON.

Sitting behind a desk in his office, Ollie is reclining in his chair, with his Chelsea booted feet on table, talking on the telephone.

> OLLIE
> Max, you're a star. That is bloody brilliant news. Fan-bloody-tastic! You won't regret it I promise you!

INT. NIGHTCLUB. WEST LONDON. NIGHT. (1964)

In a London nightclub we see Ollie breaking out the Champagne to an wildly ecstatic band.

> ROSIE (V.O.)
> As a result, Ollie managed to book the band as supporting act to Herman's Hermits in a dozen big venues in Glasgow, Manchester, Nottingham Liverpool, Leeds and London.
> (Beat)
> And to say they were excited is a wild understatement...

DANCE FLOOR.

On the dance floor, Ollie, band members & girlfriends, are dancing away to the latest sounds - all clearly enjoying themselves. Everyone is well dressed and Callum, looking very sharp in a new suit, is loving every minute.

Krys, albeit a rhythmic mover, is dancing quite ostentatiously with the sole aim of attracting as much attention as he can.

Although he is dancing with one of Hannah's friends, JULIE, Cal can't take his eyes off Hannah. She is wearing a very short figure hugging little black dress and black knee length high heeled boots.

She looks absolutely gorgeous - sexy and classy. Although fashion conscious she isn't a slave to the typical iconic sixties fashions, such as Mary Quant, etc. Hannah catches Cal looking at her and gives him a sexy wink.

                    CAL
        You look absolutely gorgeous.

                    HANNAH
        SAY AGAIN!

                    CAL
        I SAID YOU LOOK ABSOLUTELY
        GORGEOUS!!

                    HANNAH
        THANKS. YOU SCRUB UP PRETTY
        WELL YOURSELF!

                    CAL
        REALLY!?

HANNAH
REALLY.

Hannah's words are music to Cal's ears putting a big smile on his face. Having observed their brief, flirtatious exchange, Krys manoeuvres in between them, flinging his arms around her.

KRYS
(To CAL)
Hey man, your turn to get drinks... Mine's a triple malt!

Callum walks off the dance floor and approaches a drinks WAITRESS.

CAL
Hello, can I order some drinks please?

WAITRESS
Of course Sir. What can I...

Then, just as Cal is about to make the order, he is violently pushed backwards by a fat, middle aged, DRUNKEN MAN, who rudely barges between them.

Cal manages to stay on his feet but as he staggers back, he in turn bumps into a group of men standing behind him - sending their drinks flying. Aware what he has done, Cal immediately turns to apologise.

He is confronted by four hard looking men who are immaculately dressed in expensive suits. But before he gets a chance to blurt out an apology, one of them turns and looks at him with a fierce smouldering contempt.

Cal's jaw drops. To his absolute shock horror it is Bruce Gemmell - and his suit is covered in alcohol.

                    BRUCE
          You stupid prick!..
          Are you fucking blind!!

Bruce is then stopped in his tracks as he focuses on a young man who bears an uncanny resemblance to Calvin Rennie. However, before he gets the chance to say or do anything, one of his companions, FRANKIE WATTS, interjects.

> FRANKIE
> (East London)
> It wasn't his fault Bruce.
> He got pushed into us.
> I saw it.

Cal is still standing open mouthed, too gobsmacked to utter a word. Bruce stares back at him with a degree of perplexity. Although he is looking at a man of similar size and stature to Calvin Rennie, this man is masculine, well dressed and hanging out in one of London's trendiest nightclubs.

> FRANKIE (Cont'd)
> It was that fat fucker
> over there. Do you want
> me to have a word?

> BRUCE
> If you wouldn't mind
> Frankie... And see that he
> falls and breaks something.

Frankie grins and nods to one of the other burly gents. Meanwhile Bruce is still staring at Cal, but no longer with such menace.

                    BRUCE (Cont'd)
          Please accept my apologies.

                         CAL
                 (Iffy London accent)
          Eh, don't worry about it
          mate. No harm done.

                        BRUCE
                   (After beat)
          Do I know you from somewhere?

                         CAL
          Who me? No, don't think so.

The meeting is suddenly interrupted by the
appearance of two tall, dark haired burly
men, BURLY TWIN 1 and 2, dressed in smart
suits. As they walk towards Bruce they look
very pleased to see him.

                        BRUCE
                  (Offers hand to shake)
          Enjoy the rest of your
          evening.

                         CAL
                  (Shaking Bruce's hand)
          You too mate.

Bruce then turns towards the two men, who greet him and shake him warmly by the hand. Ad-lib

> ### BURLY TWIN 1
> (East London)
> Bruce! Welcome to back to London my son.

> ### BRUCE
> Thanks Ron. Great to be here.

The men put their arms around Bruce and they walk off in the direction of a private suite. As Bruce walks away he can't resist looking back at Cal one more time.

CU of Cal's shaken reaction and Krys's intrigued look.

INT. OLLIE'S MUSIC SHOP. LONDON. (1964)

The scene opens with front page of a tabloid newspaper. The banner headline reads. *SOHO GANGLAND SLAYING*! The shot pulls out to reveal Terry reading the paper. Cal, sitting opposite, is looking at the front-page headline - revealing his uneasy thoughts.

INT. MARQUEE CLUB. LONDON. NIGHT. (1965)

On stage in the Marquee club, in the heart of swinging London, the band, minus Krys, are setting up their instruments and doing sound checks, etc. Ollie looks at his watch.

> OLLIE
> Where the fuck is he?

> JEFF
> You did tell him six didn't you?

> OLLIE
> Well of course I did!

> VIC
> Perhaps he's had an accident or something.

> TERRY
> We should be so lucky.

> OLLIE
> If he's pissed again I'll bloody murder him - I swear it!

                    CAL
          There must be something
          wrong. There's no bloody way
          he's going to miss a chance
          like this.

                    TERRY
          I don't know what you're
          all so bothered about. I
          couldn't give a flying fuck if
          he never showed up again...
          Sorry Ollie, I know he's your
          cousin but let's face it,
          he's as much use to this band
          as a one legged budgie with a
          Jew's harp...

Others chuckle and laugh. Even Ollie manages
a wry smile.

                    VIC
          It's bloody true though.

Moments later, Krys appears looking very
sorry for himself.

                    TERRY
          Krys... Thank Christ, we were
          getting worried.

                    OLLIE
Where the fuck have you been?

                    KRYS
Don't hassle me man. I feel
like shit.

                    OLLIE
What do you mean 'you feel
like shit'? Have you been
drinking?!

                    KRYS
A couple — so what.

                    OLLIE
So what! What the bloody
hell did I tell you?
No booze, no drugs, no nothing!

                    KRYS
So what the fuck are they
all drinking, barley water?

                    OLLIE
At least they can all stand
up straight!

                    KRYS
          Jesus relax man. I'll be fine.
          I've just had some bad weed
          that's all...

                    OLLIE
          Listen you wanker. I've
          worked my backside off and
          pulled a lot of strings to
          get us this opportunity. If
          you think Barnaby Shand,
          of Decca records, gets off
          his skinny arse to come and
          listen to just anyone, you
          must be a bigger bloody
          tosser than you are already!

Krys, not looking all that with it, suddenly
clamps a hand over his mouth and scrambles
in the direction of the toilets.

                    OLLIE (Cont'd)
          Jesus Christ... This is all
          we need! Can one of you drag
          him across to the cafe and
          pour half a dozen coffees down
          his throat. If Shand sees
          him like this we're buggered
          before we start.

INT. CAFÉ. SOHO, LONDON. NIGHT. (1965)

In a small café near to the club, Krys, Cal and Terry are sitting at a table. Krys, is bent forward with his head buried in folded arms.

>   KRYS
>   I just wanna die man...
>   I just wanna die...

>   TERRY
>   What was it you had for
>   Christ sake?

>   KRYS
>   Fuck knows...
>   Some sort of new Hash.

>   CAL
>   I'll get him another one.

Callum gets up, walks to the counter and orders another large strong coffee. As he reaches into his jacket pocket for money, he feels a tin foil sachet.

A devious thought crosses Cal's mind. From the pocket he removes a small sachet of sleeping pills. (same ones he got at chemist) After he pays, he pops two white pills from the sachet and drops them into Kry's coffee.

INT. MARQUEE CLUB. LONDON. (1965)

The Barracuda's, minus Krys, are on stage performing a strong, up tempo track from their set. In the audience, standing next to Ollie, we focus on BARNABY SHAND, a slim, sharply dressed man who looks like a hip banker.

Ollie glances at Barnaby to judge his reaction - but he isn't giving much away.

INT. OLLIE'S MINI BUS. NIGHT. (1965)

Krys is spark out in the back of Ollie's Mini bus... snoring loudly.

INT. KRYS'S FLAT. LONDON. DAY. (1965)

In his modern but fairly untidy top floor
converted flat, a dishevelled and miffed
looking Krys Winslow is with Hannah.

> KRYS
>
> Jesus woman, have you
> listened to a bloody word
> I've said? I wasn't there, I
> wasn't part of it! As far as
> Barnaby Shand's concerned I
> don't fucking exist!...

> HANNAH
>
> And whose fault is that?

> KRYS
>
> Ok, so I got a bit wasted
> but not that wasted. Terry
> and Jock strap took me to
> some café to sober me up,
> right... I was doing fine,
> then, wallop, next thing I
> know I wake up in the back
> of the bloody mini bus...

> HANNAH
>
> So?...

                    KRYS
So! What do you mean 'so'?!
Caffeine is supposed to wake
you up, not poleaxe you for
fifteen bloody hours!...
I tell you there are some
negative vibes going down
here. Totally fucking
negative.

                    HANNAH
Krys, the only negative
vibes are in your Head.

                    KRYS
What's that supposed to mean?

                    HANNAH
You tell me. You're the one
who's perpetually shitfaced.

                    KRYS
I'm under some heavy, heavy
pressure right now. I need
stimulation to stay in touch
with my creative dimension.

                    HANNAH
The only thing you need to
stay in touch with your
creative dimension is rubber
glove and jar of Vaseline!

                    KRYS
You bitch... You fucking
bitch!

                    HANNAH
Well, what do you expect.

                    KRYS
A bit of loyalty for
starters.

                    HANNAH
Jeez that's rich coming from
you. You wouldn't know what
loyalty was if it poked your
eyes out.

                    KRYS
Oh Jesus, not that again.
I can't help it if other
chicks dig me!

HANNAH

That's it. I've had enough
of this.

KRYS

What do you expect me to do.
It's not as if I force them
to sleep with me.

HANNAH

It may surprise you to know
that other guys like me too.

Hannah walks to the front door and opens
it. As she does Krys walks up from behind
and slams it shut.

HANNAH (Cont'd)

I want to leave.

KRYS

But you've only just got
here.

HANNAH

We're finished Krys.
So please just get
out of my way.

                    KRYS
I knew it. I bloody knew
it!... Jock strap has turned
you against me... Just like
everyone else!

                    HANNAH
You've done a pretty good
job of that yourself.

                    KRYS
Ever since that tartan
tosser showed up, all
I've ever heard is Jack
so fab, Jack so cool, Jack
so groovy... Jack!, Jack!,
Jack!, Jack!, Jack!..
I fucking exist too you
know!

                    HANNAH
God you are pathetic.

Hannah reaches for the door handle again
but Krys doesn't move. He grabs her wrist
tightly.

                    KRYS
I'll show you pathetic!

INT. OLLIE'S MUSIC SHOP. LONDON. DAY. (1965)

Cal walks into Ollie's office with a sense of purpose. The first thing he sees is Ollie and Julie comforting Hannah. Julie is holding a cold wet towel against the side of Hannah's face.

Hannah looks up, revealing a swollen mouth and a blackened eye. Although her eyes are red and tearful, she still manages to put on a brave face.

                    CAL (Cont'd)
          What happened?... Who did
          this!?

INT. HALLWAY. KRYS'S APARTMENT. DAY. (1965)

Krys opens his front door. Just as it opens wide enough a hard accurate punch sends him reeling backwards onto the hallway floor. Cal then barges in and leaps onto Krys, pinning him to the ground.

> CAL
> You piece of shit!
> > (Punctuated by punches)
> If you ever lay so much as a
> finger on her again, I'll knock
> your teeth so far down your
> throat, you'll be shitting
> them for weeks!

Krys groans as he is rendered semi conscious. Cal exits.

EXT. HANNAH'S APARTMENT. NIGHT. (1965)

Callum rings the front door bell of a smart apartment. Moments later the door opens revealing Hannah - her swollen features much improved. They look at each other momentarily then embrace with great affection. Cal gently kisses the top of her head and they go inside.

INT. OLLIE'S OFFICE. LONDON. DAY. (1965)

Krys, his face swollen and bruised, is standing in Ollie's office with a look of incredulity. Ollie, sitting on the edge of his desk casually lights up a small cigar.

> KRYS
>
> What!?... What!?... You're kidding me right? I mean no way, no fucking way!...
> (Beat)
> We're cousins man, family! You made a promise to my mother. Without her you'd have nothing... Fuck all with a capital 'F'!...
> Nobody dumps Krys Winslow. I dump them!

Ollie exhales a contemptuous puff of smoke.

INT. DECCA RECORDS. LONDON. DAY. (1965)

In the impressive studios of Decca records, Cal and the band are laying down some tracks for their audition tape. In the control room, sitting at the mixing desk, is Barnaby Shand and a pensive looking Ollie.

                    ROSIE (V.O.)
          Krys was none too pleased
          at being slung out the band
          but as far as they were
          concerned, his treatment of
          Hannah was just the excuse
          they'd been waiting for.

EXT. CENTRAL LONDON LOCATION. DAY. (1965)

We see the band posing at a photo shoot.

> ROSIE (V.O. Cont'd)
>
> And the timing couldn't have been better, because Decca Records liked The Barracudas so much they signed them up right there and then.
>
> (Beat)
>
> In twelve months Cal had gone from battered rent boy to up and coming pop star... And although I have reservations about the way he's gone about it, I have to admit that faced with the same set of circumstances, I would have probably done the same.

INT. LOUNGE. KRYS'S APARTMENT. NIGHT. (1965)

We see a black and white picture of The Barracudas performing on Ready Steady Go. Shot pulls out to reveal show broadcast on a TV set. Slumped in an armchair, a dishevelled looking Krys Winslow, bottle of whiskey in hand, is watching.

A close up of Krys shows an expression of brooding envy — building like a pressure cooker.

INT. STUDIO. READY STEADY GO. (1965)

On the studio stage, RSG presenter, CATHY MCGOWAN, is interviewing Callum, AKA Jack Dallas.

> CATHY MCGOWAN
> That's a pretty lively record you've got there?

> CAL
> Thanks very much.

> CATHY MCGOWAN
> So Jack, are you the leader of the group?

                        CAL (On TV)
          No, not at all. We all muck
          in together.

                        CATHY MCGOWAN (On TV)
          But you write all the songs
          don't you?

                        CAL (On TV)
          I do but we're a team. Each
          member of the band brings
          something to the table.

INT. LOUNGE. KRYS'S APARTMENT. NIGHT. (1965)

Resume.

Krys can bear it no longer. He picks up a
bottle of Jack Daniels and throws it at the
television screen.

SERIES OF SHOTS C. (1966)

C1. CLOSE UP. MELODY MAKER SINGLES CHART.

Chart shows ******* by The Barracudas at no 1 on 17th March 1966 — pushing the Walker Brothers into second place.

C2. CLOSE UP. ALBUM COVER.

The design is a colour photo of The Barracudas posing in a London location, looking cool and relaxed. The album is called 'THE BARRACUDAS'.

> ROSIE (V.O. Cont'd)
> Following the success of
> their first two singles, Cal
> ripped off just about everyone
> he could think of and the
> band released its first L.P.

C3. CLOSE UP — MELODY MAKER ALBUM CHARTS.

The Barracuda's chart at No 3. The Rolling Stones are at 2 with 'Aftermath'. The Beatles are at No 1 with 'Revolver'.

> ROSIE (VO Cont'd)
> Suddenly the Barracuda's were pop stars. TV appearances, screaming fans, Champagne showbiz parties and cash to go with it.

C4. WEST LONDON. DAY.

We see Cal driving through west London in a bright red E-type Jaguar sports car with Hannah by his side. Both look very happy (Not smug though)

The Jaguar enters a smart west London mews and pulls up outside a very smart town house.

> ROSIE (VO Cont'd)
> And as far as Cal was concerned, life couldn't get much sweeter.

C5. INT. LOUNGE. OLLIE 'S HOUSE.

In the front lounge of a very up market west London town house, the band members, Hannah and about a dozen others, are excitedly crowded around a TV set.

A close up of the screen shows the famous forth goal by Geoff Hurst, in the 1966 world cup final. With the words, *"They thought it was all over — it is now!"*, they all go wild. Cal smiles knowingly to himself.

C6. INT. BETTING SHOP.

The miffed looking MANAGER is handing bundles of notes to Cal who is transferring the money into two very large, cash stuffed, holdalls.

> CAL
> Four goals to two.
> Who'd have guessed.

INT. OFFICE. NEWSPAPER. LONDON. NIGHT. (1966)

Hacking away on his typewriter in the office of a tabloid newspaper, KEN CHIVERS, a weedy ginger haired man, who looks much older than his thirty years, answers his phone.

                    KEN
        Ken Chivers…

INT. PHONE BOX. LONDON. DAY. (1966)

                    KRYS
        Hey Ken - How's it going man?
            (Beat)
        Krys... Krys Winslow...
        Remember?
            (Few beats)
        Eh, yeah, used to be...
        Anyway, I was wondering if
        you could do me a small
        favour?
            (Beat)
        Nothing much, just some
        poking around.

EXT. NIGHTCLUB. LONDON. NIGHT. (1966)

Two limousines pull up outside an upmarket venue in west London, where dozens of photographers are waiting. The chauffeur from the first limo opens the rear passenger door and out gets Ollie with his girlfriend JANA — followed by Cal arm in arm with Hannah.

INT. NIGHTCLUB. LONDON. NIGHT (1966)

In a trendy west end nightclub, we see Cal, Hannah, Ollie and the other band members mixing with the great and the good. A huge banner hanging from the ceiling says *'HAPPY BIRTHDAY OLLIE'*.

Rosie approaches Cal. (Unseen to others)

> ROSIE
> Got to hand it to you Cal,
> Rich and famous, gorgeous
> girlfriend, celebrity pals...
> I'm impressed mate, I really
> am.
> (Beat)
> Even if you are the biggest
> fraud in pop music history.

                    CAL
Grow a pair and get on with
it you said — remember.
        (Beat)
My whole life I've dreamed of
living like this and now I am.
And all thanks to a celestial
balls up.
        (Beat)
The only thing that spoils it
is knowing that anytime soon
I'll have to give it all up
and return to my own shitty
worthless existence.
        (Beat)
Until that sad day I'm going
to make the most of it.
Cheers...

LATER. RECEPTION.

Hannah enters the reception and approaches a smartly dressed middle aged man who is looking at some artwork.

>   HANNAH
>   Uncle Andrew!

The man turns to Hannah. It is Andrew Wishart, dressed in a dinner suit. They kiss and embrace.

>   WISHART
>   Hannah darling.
>   As beautiful as ever.

RESUME CAL.

Cal is chatting to Tom Jones and actor Michael Caine.

>   CAL
>   You know Michael, there's
>   something I've always wanted
>   to say to you.

>   MICHAEL CAINE
>   And what's that Jack?

                    CAL
            (Impersonating Mr Caine)
        Now you're a big man but
        you're out of shape. With me
        it's a full time job...
        Now behave.

Mr Caine looks totally nonplussed. (The
quote is from the film 'Get Carter' which
isn't made until 1970).

                    CAL (Cont'd)
        Never mind, you'll get it
        in a few years.

                    HANNAH
        Excuse me a moment gentlemen.
            (Beat)
        Jack, there is someone I
        would like you to meet.

When Cal (Known as Jack) turns to face
Hannah he cannot believe his eyes.

                    HANNAH (Cont'd)
        I would like to introduce
        you to my godfather. Andrew
        Wishart.

> WISHART
> Jack. What an honour it is to meet you at last. Hannah's told me so much I feel I know you already.

Cal gets a feeling in the pit of his stomach like he has just swallowed a five pound lead ball. Totally gob smacked, he must quickly pull himself together.

EXT. ALLEYWAY. SIDE OF RESTAURANT. (1966)

In a dimly lit service alleyway that runs down the side of the restaurant, a shifty looking Ken Chivers knocks on a fire exit door. Moments later the door opens and a waiter furtively beckons him in.

DANCEFLOOR.

Terry, Vic and Jeff are dancing with a posse of girls. Moments later a waiter approaches them holding a tray with a magnum of iced Champagne. We see the waiter is Ken Chivers. After serving the Champagne, Ken slips away, walking amongst the guests, slyly checking them out.

LATER. NEAR TOILETS.

Cal exits 'the gents' into a corridor. As he does, he comes face to face with Andrew Wishart.

> WISHART
> Ah, Jack, there you are.
> I've been looking for you.
> Not trying to avoid me I hope.

> CAL
> Something I can do for you
> Andrew?

> WISHART
> Just a quiet chat.

> CAL
> Oh, what about?

> WISHART
> Old friendships. Past
> acquaintances.
>   (Beat)
> Oh don't look so bewildered
> Calvin. Your miraculous
> transformation may have
> fooled everyone but it hasn't
> fooled me...

                    CAL
          I think you have me mixed
          up with somebody else.

                    WISHART
          I almost fell for it myself
          until Hannah unwittingly
          mentioned a certain
          distinctively shaped scar
          on your chest.

                    CAL
               (After beat)
          What the fuck do you want?

                    WISHART
          As I said, just a quiet
          chat... Unless of course, you
          would rather have out here.

Under the circumstances Cal is obliged to
accept. We then see that Ken Chivers has been
slyly observing them. As Cal and Wishart
exit the dining area through a door marked
'Private', Ken is compelled to follow.

Ken looks furtively around him then walks towards the door. However, just as he reaches it, a heavy hand lands on the top of his shoulder stopping him in his tracks. He turns to see a big, TIPSY GUEST, with a jovial assertive manner.

> TIPSY GUEST
> Waiter! Four large glasses of
> Champagne - there's a good
> chap!

UPSTAIRS OFFICE.

In an upstairs private office.

> WISHART
> I have to hand it to you
> Calvin... Lead singer in a
> highly successful pop group,
> a gorgeous girlfriend, fame,
> fortune, celebrity chums. It
> really is hard to believe...
> As I recall you could hardly
> whistle.

> CAL
> Is this going somewhere?

WISHART

For me alas, fortune hasn't been so kind. One minute one has respect and position, the next, cast aside and rejected.

(Beat)

All except for Hannah of course. Beautiful, bright, dear sweet Hannah. It must be most gratifying to receive the adoration of such an extraordinary young woman...

(Beat)

However, I wonder how long it would last if the world was to discover the sordid truth about your less than glorious past...

DINING AREA/STAIRWELL.

Ken Chivers once again moves towards the door marked private. He slyly looks about to see if anyone is watching then opens the door and walks through.

After closing the door behind him, Ken finds that he is at the bottom of a stairwell that leads up to rooms/offices on the floor above. He creeps up the stairs.

UPSTAIRS OFFICE.

Resume Callum and Wishart.

>   WISHART
>   A vulgar, but well funded
>   newspaper, has offered me
>   an obscene amount to tell
>   my story. You know, naming
>   names, my prison hell, etc...
>   (Beat)
>   Can you see where I'm going
>   now.

STAIRWELL/UPSTAIRS LANDING.

Ken Chivers is now near the top of the stairs. Although there is sound from the music below, he can hear the voices of Cal and Wishart coming from one of the two offices. But in order to hear what is being said clearly he must get right up to the office door — which is slightly ajar.

>   CAL (From office)
>   This is bollocks,
>   total bollocks!

>   WISHART (From office)
>   Talk about shit hitting the fan.

>   CAL (From office)
>   We never had a relationship. The
>   first time I ever set eyes on you
>   was outside the hospital!

Listening at the door Ken is intrigued by what he hears. Suddenly the door at the bottom of the stairs opens, blasting music up the stairwell. As it closes, Ken hears giggling and footsteps coming up the stairs. Desperate not to be caught he frantically looks for a place to hide.

UPSTAIRS OFFICE.

Cal hears the giggling couple reach the landing at the top of the stairs and gestures Wishart to be quiet.

The couple turn out to be Terry and a female friend. They go into another room on the opposite side of the landing. Cal then closes shut the office door.

> CAL
> You can say what you like,
> I'll deny everything! Who are
> they going to believe anyway?
> Me, or a twisted old shirt
> lifter who's just done time
> for perjury!

From his inside his jacket pocket, Wishart produces a photograph.

> WISHART
> They might believe this
> though.

A close up reveals it to be a copy of a photo they had taken together in Carnaby St. Cal looks absolutely mortified.

                    WISHART (Cont'd)
          You can keep it if you like.
          I have lot's more.

                         CAL
          This isn't me. It's somebody
          else!

                       WISHART
          Looks like you to me... Either
          way, your career and love life
          will dissolve quicker than a
          sugar cube in a mug of steaming
          hot tea.

Cal's stunned reaction.

                    WISHART (Cont'd)
          However, for a small
          remuneration no one
          need be any the wiser.

UPSTAIRS LANDING.

Between the two offices we focus on a door.
It creaks open revealing Ken Chivers hiding
in a broom cupboard. Satisfied that the coast
is clear, he sneaks out and creeps over
to carry on eavesdropping. To his further
frustration the door is now fully closed
and all he can hear is the murmur of voices.
He strains to hear.

UPSTAIRS OFFICE.

Resume Cal and Wishart.

>   CAL
>   FIFTEEN GRAND?!

>   WISHART
>   Considering the circumstances
>   I think it's quite
>   reasonable.

>   CAL
>   Reasonable! You taking the piss!

>   WISHART
>   The rate for someone in your
>   position is far higher.

                    CAL
    Oh well, that's alright then.
    For a twisted blackmailing
    shitbag you're just so
    generous.

                    WISHART
    Call it a family discount...

UPSTAIRS LANDING.

Outside the office, Ken Chivers spots an air
vent high up on the wall. Through the vent
he can hear Cal and Wishart but he is too
low to make out what is being said.

Ken then looks quickly about for something
to stand on. Next to the wall outside the
other office is a wooden chair.

UPSTAIRS OFFICE.

Resume Cal and Wishart.

>   WISHART
> Are you are willing to risk
> everything you have achieved
> over a paltry fifteen thousand?
>   (Beat)
> And when the authorities
> discover your involvement
> in a treasonous conspiracy
> to sell top secret defence
> information to the Soviets,
> you will also face life
> behind bars.

>   CAL
> What! What Conspiracy!?
> The Soviets!? Treason!?
> What the fuck are you on
> about!?

UPSTAIRS LANDING.

Ken picks up the chair, puts it down under
the vent and stands on it. Now with his ear
level with the vent he can now hear clearly
what is being said.

>   WISHART (Through vent)
> Don't tell me you've
> conveniently forgotten about
> that as well.

>   CAL (Through vent)
> Forgotten about what? I don't
> know what you're on about!
> It's total bollocks just like
> everything else!

>   WISHART (Through vent)
> In that case I suggest you
> talk to your old chum Bruce
> Gemmell... That's if he
> doesn't put a bullet through
> your head first...
>   (Beat)
> Yes, I know all about him
> too.

Although he has missed all of the juicy bits, Ken is very intrigued. Seconds later, footsteps approach the door from within the office. Ken immediately steps down off the chair and creeps down the stairs.

RESUME UPSTAIRS OFFICE.

Wishart is just about to exit.

> WISHART
> I'm off to visit an old friend
> for a couple of weeks. I'll
> contact you on my return.
>> (Beat)
> Super party by the way. We
> must do it again sometime.

The mention of Bruce Gemmell is devastating.
Wishart exits leaving Cal looking stunned,
dejected and very worried.

EXT. PARK. CENTRAL LONDON. DAY. (1966)

Cal and Rosie are sitting together on a park bench.

> CAL
>
> How the bloody hell was I supposed to know Hannah was Wishart's goddaughter?

> ROSIE
>
> I take it you're going to pay him then.

> CAL
>
> What choice have I got.

> ROSIE
>
> Look, if it's any consolation, Calvin was what he was but he was no traitor.

EXT. KELVINSIDE. GLASGOW. NIGHT. (1964)

Calvin Rennie leaves an upmarket apartment. Waiting on the other side of the street is Bruce Gemmell's Jaguar.

> ROSIE (V.O.)
> Bruce found out about Wishart's fondness for young men and came up with a plan to use Calvin to steal secret defence info that Wishart had access to.

As Calvin Rennie walks along a dimly lit street, he is jumped from behind, a cloth sack is put over his head and he is roughly bundled into the boot of Bruce's car.

INT. OUTBUILDING. DAY. (1964)

In a dimly lit, empty outbuilding with a concrete floor, a hooded and soaking wet Calvin Rennie, is kneeling down in a military style stress position - shivering with cold and fear.

A grinning Archie Gemmell then steps forward and pours a bucket of ice cold water over him, causing him to gasp. Bruce then approaches and removes his hood.

> ROSIE (V.O.)
> Bruce made him an offer he
> couldn't refuse.

INT. UPMARKET APARTMENT. GLASGOW. NIGHT. (1964)

In the bathroom, Andrew Wishart is enjoying a shower. Whilst he does, we see Calvin Rennie, dressed in a bathrobe, furtively entering a study.

He sneaks over to a large desk and from underneath it pulls out a leather briefcase. He opens the case and pulls out a couple of folders marked 'M.O.D. TOP SECRET'.

> ROSIE (V.O. Cont'd)
> Gemmell had done a deal
> with some Russian to supply
> detailed info on a nuclear
> Sub base. Wishart carried the
> documents in his briefcase,
> so all Calvin had to do was
> steal them.

Calvin quickly opens one of them and studies it for a few moments.

A close up reveals the document to be a detailed map of a Royal Navy nuclear submarine base in the west of Scotland. Calvin then closes the folder and tucks it into his bathrobe.

ROSIE (V.O. Cont'd)
Unfortunately that's when it
all went a bit Pete Tong.

EXT. FISHING VILLAGE. SCOTLAND. DAY. (1964)

The Gemmell brothers are standing by their
car which is parked on the quayside of a
remote Scottish fishing village.

Moments later a small motor boat, with three
men aboard, moors at the quay.

ARCHIE
Fifteen grand here we come!

One of them, YURI, best described as a
Soviet Captain Birdseye, is assisted out of
the boat by a tough looking comrade. The
third man remains in the boat.

BRUCE
Yuri — how's it going?

As Yuri approaches, he bluntly thrusts the
M.O.D. folder, that Calvin stole, into
Bruce's hands.

                    YURI
          This is NOT what I ask for!

                    BRUCE
          What!?

                    YURI
          I asked for detailed
          information!

                    BRUCE.
          It's the plans to the sub base
          you asked for. What's the
          problem?

                    YURI
          They are out of date! This
          not show latest defences and
          silo position. Without this
          they are useless! And until
          I get exactly what I ask
          there will be no money!

Bruce is absolutely furious. His rage
smoulders.

EXT. PARK. CENTRAL LONDON. DAY. (1966)

Resume Cal and Rosie.

> CAL
> So Calvin took the wrong
> plans from Wishart's
> briefcase?

> ROSIE
> An easy mistake. Needless
> to say Bruce didn't quite
> see it that way.

EXT. CROWN ST BRIDGE. GLASGOW. NIGHT (1964)

Archie and Bobby Gemmell are removing the
battered, bloodied and motionless body of
Calvin from the boot of Bruce's car.

> BOBBY
> Oh, Jesus... I'm having
> no more part in this.

> ARCHIE
> You either help or you don't.
> But hell mend you when Bruce
> finds out!

Bobby reluctantly lends a hand. They then carry Calvin to the parapet of the bridge, lift him up and shove him off down into the water.

EXT. PARK. CENTRAL LONDON. DAY. (1966)

Resume Cal and Rosie.

> ROSIE
> Calvin wasn't supposed to
> die. The cold water revived
> him and he could have
> survived.
> But the sad truth is he'd had
> enough and decided to let go...
> The rest you know.

EXT. PUB. GLASGOW. NIGHT. (1966)

In their local pub, The Auld Shank, the Gemmell's are enjoying a drink.

> ARCHIE
> (To Bobby)
> So what sort of crap do you get up to at these acting classes then?

> BOBBY
> All sorts really. Tonight we spent the whole lesson on mime.

> BRUCE
> Mime. Like that irritating French fucker.

> BOBBY
> In one exercise we had to pretend we were walking through a field full of flowers, spider webs and syrup.

> ARCHIE
> Sounds a right load of bollocks.

> BOBBY
> That's so bloody typical of
> you two. If it's got nothing
> to do with football, women or
> booze you're not interested.

> BRUCE
> Believe me wee brother, if
> you want to mince about like
> a soft shite, good luck to
> you...
> But in this neighbourhood
> you might want to keep it
> to yourself.

Moments later Bruce is approached by a huge
bruiser, BIG TAM.

> BIG TAM
> Bruce, got some jessie here
> from London... Says he
> wants to speak with you.

Bruce and his brothers look curious. Big
Tam beckons someone (Out of shot). The
person comes forward. It is Krys Winslow,
totally intimidated but trying his best
not to show it.

                    KRYS
         Hi... eh, I have some
         information about someone I
         believe you are looking for.

                    BRUCE
         And who would that be?

                    KRYS
         Calvin Rennie.

Bruce is very surprised but deliberately
plays it cool. Bob and Archie however, show
more reaction.

                    KRYS (Cont'd)
         I know where he is, and for
         two hundred pounds, I'll
         gladly share the information.

Reaction Bob & Archie. Bruce gestures them
to stay quiet.

                    BRUCE
         Thing is, we already know
         everything there is to
         know about Mr Rennie. So
         unfortunately it would seem
         you've had a wasted journey.

As Krys hits the buffers, Bob and Archie look as equally perplexed. What is Bruce playing at?

> KRYS
> (Crestfallen)
> Oh... eh, everything?

> BRUCE
> Where he lives, where he goes. Even his favourite brand of lavvy paper.

> KRYS
> (A few beats)
> Oh... oh I see.
> (Awkward pause)
> I, eh.. I guess I'll, eh, be on my way then.

> BRUCE
> However, as you've come such a long way, I'll make you a offer... If you can tell me something I don't already know about Rennie, I'll give you thirty pounds.

                    KRYS
          Eh, okay, fair enough... So I
          take it you already know he's
          Jack Dallas... The pop star.

Suddenly the Brothers 'so what' demeanour
changes to one of incredulity. They think
about it then burst out laughing. Ad-lib
comments, etc.

                    BRUCE
          I'm not paying you for shit
          you've made up.

                    KRYS
          But I'm not making it up.
          Honest. I got it from a very
          reliable source.

                    BRUCE
          And who would that be?

                    KRYS
          Some bloke I know.

                    ARCHIE
          Sounds like he's taken you
          for a right cunt.

                    KRYS
     I swear it man, it's no joke!
     This guy is straight up. He's
     a crime reporter called Ken
     Chivers...
          (Beat)
     He was working under-cover as
     a waiter at Ollie Jackson's
     birthday bash when he
     overheard an argument between
     Dallas and some posh bloke
     called Wishart - who kept
     calling Dallas 'Calvin'...

The name Wishart wipes the smile off the
Brother's faces.

                    KRYS (Cont'd)
     He didn't hear enough to find
     out what it was all about but
     your name was mentioned.

                    BRUCE
     My name!? And what makes him
     so sure they were talking
     about me?

                    KRYS
Eh, let's just say that your
reputation is just as well
known down south as it is
elsewhere.

                    BRUCE
Is that right... Well you
tell your nosey reporter
friend this!... The
Calvin Rennie we know
is a talentless, limp
wristed little turd, who
makes Liberace look like
Sparticus...
        (Beat)
And the notion that he has
magically transformed himself
into Jack Dallas, is the most
ridiculous pile of shite I
have ever heard!...
        (Beat)
And more importantly, just
because he heard a name, that
just happens to be the same
as mine, it is very fucking
dangerous to assume that it
is me!... Do I make myself
clear?

Bruce pulls a five pound note from his pocket and throws it on the table.

> BRUCE (Cont'd)
> That's for your fare home.
> Now fuck off while you still
> can...

Krys quickly exits with tail firmly between his legs, leaving the Gemmell's looking shell shocked as they digest the news about Calvin Rennie, AKA Jack Dallas.

> ARCHIE
> Un — fucking - believable!...
> You give the bastard brain
> damage and it turns him into
> a fucking pop star...

> BOBBY
> I told you there was
> something different about him.

> BRUCE
> I knew it was him in London.
> I fucking knew it!

They ponder momentarily.

                    BRUCE (Cont'd)
       As if Wishart's not bad
       enough now we've got this
       fucking reporter to worry
       about. Question is, how much
       do they know and what are
       they up to?

INT. CAR. STREET. LONDON. DAY. (1966)

Inside a parked car, Krys is talking with
Ken Chivers.

                    KEN
       You wanker! I explicitly
       told you not to mention me
       by name. What are you trying
       to do, get me killed?

                    KRYS
       Two hundred quid you said...
       What did I get, a fucking
       fiver...
            (Beat)
       I wouldn't mind but the train
       fare cost me six pound fifty!

KEN

Shit! If Gemmell doesn't
go after Dallas I've got
nothing. No story, no glory.

KRYS

Dallas is hiding something,
I bet my life on it... What
about a story on him and
Wishart? 'The poof and the
Pop star'...
That's bound to stir a bit of
shit.

KEN

Jesus - for the last time.
All I heard was parts of a
heated conversation. Wishart
is Dallas's girlfriend's
Godfather. So they argued,
so what!?... It's hardly the
scoop of the fucking century
is it!

KRYS

(After beat)
You're supposed to be a
bloody journalist. Can't you
just make something up?

INT. CAL'S HOUSE. LONDON. EVE. (1966)

In the spacious lounge Hannah is sitting on a high stool, working behind an angled draughtsman's/designers drawing table. Cal approaches and stands over her shoulder. We see that she is a talented illustrator. Cal looks impressed and complements her. Moments later the doorbell rings.

FRONT DOOR.

Through the peep hole we see a fish eye view of Andrew Wishart. Cal's heart sinks. However, he opens the door.

> WISHART
> Ah, Jack... I was hoping you were in.

> CAL
> What do you want?.

> WISHART
> Just passing... Wondered how you both were.

> CAL
> We're fine... Anything else?

Hannah suddenly comes to the door. She kisses and embraces Wishart.

> HANNAH
> Uncle Andrew, I thought it was you! Come in, come in.

> WISHART
> How are you my dear. I was in the area so I thought I'd pop by and say hello...

LOUNGE. LATER.

Wishart is sitting on a large sofa. Hannah walks over and hands him a glass of port. Cal, sitting on the chair opposite, looks very ill at ease.

> WISHART (Cont'd)
> So Jack, how are things in the exciting world of pop music?

> CAL
> Not bad.

                    WISHART
Hannah tells me you have been
busy writing some new tunes
for the bands forthcoming
L.P.?

                    CAL
That's right.

                    WISHART
I must say I envy you.
Creative fulfilment and plenty
of cash to boot. What more
could a man want.
        (Pause)
You know, sitting here you
bear an uncanny resemblance
to a young acquaintance of
mine.

Callum almost chokes on his drink and begins
to cough.

                    WISHART (Cont'd)
His name is Calvin Rennie,
from Drumchapel. I don't
suppose you have any family
over that way?

                    CAL
No I don't.

                  WISHART
Just as well. Frightful
place.
          (uncomfortable pause)
So what did you do before you
came to London?

                    CAL
Eh, nothing much. Bit of bar
work, labouring, that sort of
thing.

                  HANNAH
Jack's isn't too keen about
sharing his past. Sometimes
I think I know more about the
man on the moon.

                    CAL
I told you I was brought up
in an orphanage, there isn't
much to tell.

                    WISHART
        Well, with such a bright
        future ahead, I suppose
        there's little point in
        trawling up the past —
        don't you agree?

Cal/Jack's very uncomfortable reaction.

INT. PHONE BOX. GLASGOW. DAY. (1966)

Bruce Gemmell talking on phone in a public
phone box.

                    BRUCE
        And you're sure Wishart
        lives there?
             (Few beats)
        And what about this Ken
        Chivers?
             (Few beats)
        Fuck! I don't like it. He
        sounds like trouble...
             (Few beats)
        It's okay, I'll take care of it.
             (Beat)
        Thanks Frankie. I owe you
        pal. Cheers.

EXT. WEST LONDON. NIGHT. (1966)

It is late evening and it is raining steadily. An Austin Mini car pulls up and parks in an upmarket residential street. The driver, dressed in a duffle coat, buttoned right up to the neck and wearing dark glasses, gets out and looks warily about him.

He then picks up a brown paper wrapped package from the passenger seat, pulls the hood of the duffle coat over his head and begins to walk along the street.

We then see the same man walking up some steps to the pillared (illuminated) entrance of a grand town house. The curtains to the lower storey lounge window are partially drawn allowing lamp light and the flickering of a television set to be seen. The man furtively looks about him then rings the doorbell. Moments later the door is opened by Andrew Wishart.

> WISHART
> Well look who it is.

STUDY.

As the man is led into a small study he pulls down the hood of his coat and removes his glasses. He then thrusts the package into Wishart's hands.

> CAL
> Count it. It's all there.

> WISHART
> Ah, another contribution to
> my retirement fund... A wise
> and sensible choice dear boy.

> CAL
> Like I had one.

> WISHART
> Believe me, the alternative
> would be far more ruinous.
> This way you're secret is
> safe and sound.

> CAL
> I hope for your sake that
> it will be. Now if you don't
> mind there's somewhere else
> I'd rather be.

                    WISHART
        Leaving so soon. I thought
        we could have a drink -
        for old times.

                     CAL
        I don't think so.

Seconds later the front doorbell rings.

                    WISHART
        Oh. I wonder who that could
        be. Excuse me a moment.

HALLWAY.

Andrew Wishart walks out of the study and
into the hallway to answer the front door.
He then opens the door.

                 WISHART (O.S.)
        Can I help you?

STUDY.

BANG!! A shotgun blast makes Cal jump out of his skin. Seconds later there is another blast. Cal dare not move or make a sound. He then hears hurried footsteps followed seconds later by the roar of a motorcycle as it speeds away.

Moments later, Cal finds the courage to investigate and tentatively peeks around the door into the hallway. The sight that confronts him makes him gasp. Andrew Wishart's body is lying motionless in an increasing pool of blood.

HALLWAY.

With a degree of caution, Cal moves closer to see if there are any signs of life. Such is the severe nature of Wishart's wounds it is obvious that he is dead.

Cal is absolutely stunned and sits on the stairs to regain his composure. Then, realising that the front door is wide open, he springs to his feet and switches off the hall light. As he does this he hears approaching voices.

As quietly as possible, Cal tiptoes his way towards the kitchen in the expectation that there is a rear exit. Just as he reaches the kitchen door he suddenly remembers the package of cash. He then gingerly runs back, enters the study and quickly grabs it.

KITCHEN.

In the large kitchen Cal makes his way to the back door which he finds locked — with no key. With the voices now nearing the front door he begins to panic and starts looking for a key.

HALLWAY.

At the front door a MIDDLE AGED COUPLE walking their dog, drawn by the shotgun blast, walk up to the illuminated porch, push open the ajar front door and discover Wishart's blood spattered body.

KITCHEN.

Back in the kitchen, Cal hears a horrified female scream and a man's voice stress "Oh dear God!" His search to find the key becomes more frantic. He then spots several keys hanging on a short row of hooks fixed to the kitchen wall - but which one?

Cal quickly grabs a handful of keys. He fumbles with the first key — no good, the second. He hears the man in the hallway shout "Call the police!!" and his panic becomes more intense. Another key... It fits but will not turn.

HALLWAY.

The woman's screams have attracted the attention of others and a SECOND MAN has joined the scene. Leading away from the body, on the light coloured hallway carpet, he notices a trail of bloody footprints heading towards to the kitchen. With trepidation he decides to investigate. As he creeps towards the kitchen he can hear the squeaky rattle of someone trying a door lock.

> SECOND MAN
> Is anyone there?

As the man reaches the kitchen he hears the kitchen door slamming shut - but no one is there.

GARDEN.

As Cal bolts through the darkness of the back garden, the kitchen light is switched on partially illuminating his way. At the end of the garden is a high brick wall (approx 10ft) with jagged glass set in at the top. There is no gate so Cal has no choice but to climb over.

Callum desperately looks about for a way over the wall. He notices at the back corner a small tree but just as he moves towards it the kitchen door flies open and the man following him runs out into the garden.

SECOND MAN
YOU THERE – STOP!!

Needing both hands free to climb, Cal hastily throws the package over the wall and scrambles up the tree to the top of the wall, gashing his hand quite deeply on the jagged glass as he does.

However, just as he is high enough to be clear of the wall, Cal's foot is grabbed by the chasing man who tries to pull him down. After a couple of tugs Cal manages to yank his foot free and kick the man hard in the face.

He then scrambles up the tree and once clear of the jagged glass, drops himself from a branch down into a dark alleyway and runs.

INT. CAR. WEST LONDON. NIGHT. (1966)

Callum parks the Mini and switches off the
engine. He takes off the hood and glasses,
slouches back in the seat and blows a deep
sigh of relief.

He looks at the palm of his hand, wrapped
in a blood soaked handkerchief. After a few
moments his thoughts turn and he looks at
the brown paper parcel on seat beside him.
Although still in shock, he can't believe
his luck.

INT. CAL'S HOUSE. WEST LONDON. DAY. (1966)

We see Hannah crying on the sofa being
comforted by Callum with his arms around
her. (His cut hand properly bandaged)

EXT. TOWER BLOCK. EAST LONDON. NIGHT. (1966)

Having parked his car, we see a tipsy Ken
Chivers walking towards the entrance of a
council tower block. *(Ref: Brunswick Close
Estate, Islington, circa 1958)*

INT. TOWER BLOCK. EAST LONDON. NIGHT. (1966)

Once inside, Ken makes immediately for the lifts. To his annoyance, a sign has been taped up on the lift doors stating *'OUT OF ORDER'* He curses then makes his way to the stairwell.

STAIRWELL.

A few flights up Ken is beginning to struggle. As he climbs the last remaining steps he becomes aware of a man on the landing above. The man is Bruce Gemmell.

> BRUCE
>
> Well, if it isn't 'keyhole Ken'.

> KEN
>
> Who... Who are you?

> BRUCE
>
> Bruce Gemmell. I believe you have an interest in my career.

A split second after he gasps in terror, Bruce quickly grabs hold of Ken's head and twists it violently, breaking the neck. As Ken's body goes limp, Bruce lets it fall all the way to the bottom of the stairs. He then walks down, casually stepping over the twisted corpse.

> BRUCE (Cont'd)
> How's that for a breaking story...

On the way out, Bruce tears the 'Out of order' sign off the lift doors, screws it up, tosses it away and exits.

EXT. CAL'S HOUSE. WEST LONDON. DAY. (1966)

Outside the front door of their west London mews house we see Cal and Hannah. She opens the door of her convertible sports car (Roof up) and puts in a weekend travel bag. She and Cal then hug and kiss with great affection. Ad-lib goodbyes etc.

> CAL
> Promise you'll ring the minute you get there okay.

                        HANNAH
        I will. Love you.

Hannah then gets into the car, and drives
away, giving a wave as she goes.

INT. DECCA RECORDS. LONDON. DAY. (1966)

The Barracudas are in the studio rehearsing
a new track. It is now late 1966 and the
psychedelic era is under way. Cal decides
it is time for 'Are you gonna go my way.'
by Lenny Kravitz (or other suitable track)

Wall clock showing time (14.25) blends into
shot of same clock showing time at (19.10)
The same group, plus PRODUCER and SOUND
ENGINEER, are listening to the day's work.
We see Cal look at his watch – something is
preoccupying him. Moments later the phone
rings. The engineer answers.

                    SOUND ENGINEER
        Jack, call for you mate.

                        CAL
        About time. Cheers.
            (Picks up phone)
        Hello....

INT. PHONE BOX. RURAL AREA. NIGHT. (1966)

In a public telephone Bruce Gemmell talks
into receiver.

> BRUCE
> Hey sugar plum — long time.

INTERCUT.

The sound of Bruce Gemmell's voice stuns Cal.

> CAL
> Eh, sorry, you've got the
> wrong number.

> BRUCE
> I don't think so Rennie.

> CAL
> Listen I don't know how you
> got this number but don't
> call again, alright.

Callum hangs up. Clearly shaken by Bruce's
voice he ponders the situation. Moments
later the phone rings again.

                    CAL (Cont'd)
Hannah! Oh thank Christ...
What's taken you so long.
I've been worried sick...
What's the matter!?...
Hannah!...

                    BRUCE
I got your attention now.

                    CAL
Oh Jesus, NO!...

                    BRUCE
Oh, yes... and if you don't
do exactly what I say, sugar
lips here will end up just
like her dear old uncle
Andrew...
        (Hangs up)

                    CAL
Gemmell! GEMMELL!! ...
Hello!!

EXT. PHONE BOX. RURAL AREA. NIGHT. (1966)

Bruce exits the phone box, walks a few yards
to a green ex army Land Rover and gets in
the front passenger door.

INT. LAND ROVER.

As Bob drives the Land Rover away, Bruce turns
and looks into the rear of the vehicle. There
we see Archie Gemmell, grinning deviously
at a terrified Hannah, who is lying on the
vehicle floor, bound and gagged.

EXT. COTTAGE. DARTMOOR. ENGLAND. DAY. (1966)

Exterior location shot revealing a lonely
white cottage situated in a remote area of
Dartmoor, in Devon, south west England. It
is late November/early December.

INT. BATHROOM. COTTAGE. DARTMOOR. DAY. (1966)

Still trussed up, Hannah is lying flat on her back in a large old fashioned bath tub. Standing above her, pointing a Polaroid camera is Bobby with Archie beside him, illuminating the scene with a lamp.

Flash — Bob takes the photo.

> ARCHIE
>
> What is it with these fucking photos. If we want to show how serious we are why don't we just slice her nose and ears off?

> BOBBY
>
> What!

> ARCHIE
>
> It'll be ten times more effective than a poxy Polaroid.

> BRUCE
>
> Don't talk shite. Dallas wants his girlfriend back, not the Bride of Frankenstein.

INT. CAL'S HOUSE. WEST LONDON. DAY. (1966)

The first thing we see is a big close up of the Polaroid photograph of Hannah tied up in the bath. Shot pulls out to reveal a shocked Ollie looking at it.

> CAL
> They want twenty five grand in used notes, or they'll turn on the taps and leave her to drown.

> OLLIE
> What sort of people would do this!

> CAL
> I've got two days to come up with the money.

> OLLIE
> Jack you have got to call the Police.

> CAL
> No way!...

> OLLIE
> But why not!?

                    CAL
Because they said they would
kill her!

                    OLLIE
Well they're bound to say
that. They're hardly going
to threaten her with a
feather fucking duster.

                    CAL
I don't care I'm not risking it.

                    OLLIE
But they've got officers
specially trained in this
sort of thing... At least
we should talk to them?

                    CAL
NO!... They said not to
and that's exactly what
I'm going to do.

                    OLLIE
So you're simply going to
do whatever they say...
What if they kill you too.
Then what?

>   CAL
>   That's a chance I'm going
>   to have to take.

INT. COTTAGE. DARTMOOR. NIGHT. (1966)

In the lounge in front of a roaring log
fire, Bruce is relaxing on a tatty old sofa,
watching 'Till death do us part' on TV and
drinking beer. He laughs out loud.

HALLWAY.

Archie exits the bathroom into the hallway
(that links all of the rooms). We then see
him look slyly about him before he opens a
door and enters a room.

BEDROOM.

In a sparsely furnished and dimly lit
bedroom, Hannah is lying on a bed still
bound, gagged & trembling with cold. Archie
enters like a child entering a sweetshop.
After quietly closing the door he creeps
over to her.

> ARCHIE
> Ooh it's a bit cold in here.

Archie then places a hand on one of Hannah's
thighs and begins to stroke it — causing
her distress.

> ARCHIE (Cont'd)
> Looks like you could do with
> some warming up.

Suddenly the bedroom door opens and in walks
Bobby, carrying a plate of sandwiches and a
glass of orange juice.

> BOBBY
> What are you doing?

> ARCHIE
> Nothing. Just checking.

                    BOBBY
        Jesus, it's freezing in here.

Bobby puts down the food. He then removes
Hannah's gag and starts to untie her — to
her obvious relief.

                    ARCHIE
        What the are you doing?

                    BOBBY
        What's it look like.

                    ARCHIE
        You gone soft in the head...

Bobby ignores Archie and carries on untying
Hannah.

                ARCHIE (Cont'd)
        BRUCE, IN HERE — QUICK!

Moments later Bruce appears at the door.

                    BRUCE
        What?

                    ARCHIE
        Look what he's doing.

                    BOBBY
For God's sake Bruce we can't
keep her in here like this,
it's bloody freezing. Any
longer and she'll end up with
pneumonia, then what.

                    ARCHIE
Aw, what a shame...
Unfortunately for sugar lips
she's been kidnapped. I say
she stays in here — tied up!

                    BOBBY
Bruce please. If anyone
treated a dog like this you
would kick the shite out of
them!

                    BRUCE
Fair enough. But any daft
attempts to escape and she's
straight back in here like
Harriet Houdini at an S and M
night.

Hannah, so relieved at being untied,
unconditionally nods in agreement.

                    ARCHIE
        I don't believe this.
        One blubbery sob story and
        you turn into as big a soft
        bastard as he is!

                    BRUCE
        Why don't you shut the fuck
        up and stick the kettle on.

INT. CAL'S HOUSE. WEST LONDON. DAY. (1966)

On the coffee table in Cal's lounge is an
unzipped holdall. Within it is a strong
clear plastic bag containing neat piles of
bank notes. Cal is then revealed sitting on
his sofa waiting anxiously for the telephone
to ring.

Ollie is also there, pacing up and down in
front of the fireplace, holding a glass of
whiskey. Ollie puts down the glass and takes
out a cigarette case from his jacket inside
pocket. He opens it, takes out a cigarette
and puts it into his mouth. Cal notices but
is too anxious to care. Seeing this, Ollie
immediately removes the cigarette and puts
it back in the case.

Seconds later the phone rings and Cal jumps like a coiled spring.

                    CAL
        Gemmell...

EXT. CAL'S HOUSE. WEST LONDON. DAY. (1966)

It is very early in the morning and still dark. Callum, dressed in suitable winter clothing, opens the boot of his E-type Jaguar car and puts the holdall containing the ransom money within. Ollie is there to see him off.

                    OLLIE
        Are you sure you don't want
        me to come with you?

                    CAL
        Thanks but this is something
        I have to do on my own.

                    OLLIE
            (After beat)
        In that case I insist you
        take this.

From his jacket pocket Ollie produces a small .22 calibre pistol. Surprised, Cal hesitates for a moment.

                    OLLIE (Cont'd)
          To help even the odds.

Cal takes the gun and puts it in his pocket. The pair then shake hands and embrace.

                    OLLIE (Cont'd)
          For Christ sake take care.

                    CAL
          We've got an album to finish
          remember.

Callum, although fraught with worry, manages a smile and a small wave. He then gets into his car, starts the engine and drives away.

EXT. SOUTH/SOUTH WEST ENGLAND. DAY. (1966)

Cal is driving as fast as he can along a major route west out of London. (A4) At every opportunity he overtakes — revving the engine to the max. He passes a road sign for the town of Marlborough. We then see him driving very quickly along a country road and turn at a road sign for the village of East Kennet.

In the centre of the village we see him (wearing sunglasses) outside a telephone box, becoming increasingly frustrated whilst an elderly lady natters away. The second she finishes, he barges in, picks up the phone book and feverishly flicks through the pages.

Approximately three quarters through the book he finds a folded note cello taped to one of the pages. The note has '*RENNIE*' written on it. Cal tears it out the book and opens it. A close up reveals a set of instructions.

Back in his car, on A4 near Bristol, Cal turns onto the A38 towards Taunton. In another small town he enters a sub-post office and anxiously approaches the counter.

                    CAL
          My name is Callum Rennie.
          A letter has been left for
          me?

INT. LOUNGE. COTTAGE. DARTMOOR. DAY. (1966)

Looking uncomfortable and worried, Hannah is sitting alone in the lounge. Bobby walks in carrying a small suitcase. He gives it to her.

                    HANNAH
          Thank you.

                    BOBBY
          Good job you had it with you.

                    HANNAH
          I was going to visit my
          sister in Norwich...
          before...

                    BOBBY
        Ach, hopefully it'll be all
        over soon. Just stay cool and
        hang in there, eh.

Bobby's calm and friendly demeanour is of
great comfort. Bruce then walks in with
Archie. (Dressed in winter clothing)

                    BRUCE
        You ready Bob?

                    BOBBY
           Aye.

                    BRUCE
              (To Archie)
        We shouldn't be too long.
        Whatever you do don't let her
        out of your sight.

Bruce and Bob then exit the cottage. Moments
later we hear the Land Rover start and drive
away. Archie pulls back the lounge curtains
and watches as it leaves. As the noise
of the engine fades into the distance, he
smirks deviously.

EXT. RURAL ROAD. NR DARTMOOR. DAY. (1966)

On a rural 'B' road, we see Cal make a quick turn onto a 'C' road. Within a few hundred yards he finds his car stuck behind a tractor. Becoming more stressed by the minute, Cal recklessly overtakes, scraping the side of his car and almost loses control.

INT. COTTAGE. DARTMOOR. DAY. (1966)

In the bathroom, Hannah is drying herself off with a towel and applying some talc, etc. We notice that she is a little tearful.

In the hallway, just outside the ajar bathroom door, Archie is lurking. He creeps up to the door and peers through a small gap, just allowing him to see Hannah's shapely figure reflected in a mirror.

He carries on watching her as she puts on her bra and tight, figure hugging roll neck sweater. Moments later, as she exits the bathroom into the hallway, an arm is suddenly thrust around her neck, as Archie grabs her from behind.

                    ARCHIE
            You took your time didn't you?

As Hannah tenses, Archie sniffs her neck and
hair.

                    ARCHIE (Cont'd)
            Hmmm!... You smell dead sexy
            though.

                    HANNAH
            You're hurting me. Let go creep!

Archie then grabs one of Hannah's arms and
twists it behind her back.

                    ARCHIE
            Creep. I'll give you creep
            you stuck up bitch!

Fearing what Archie might do next, Hannah
summons the courage to fight back. She's able
to turn a little, lift up a foot and stamp
down the heel of her boot, hard onto Archie's
foot. As he yells in agony, Hannah manages
to break free and runs towards the kitchen.

                    ARCHIE (Cont'd)
            YOU FUCKING BITCH!!...

KITCHEN.

Hannah runs into the kitchen and makes straight for the back door in a bid to escape. However, she finds it locked. She tries again but it will not budge.

Moments later the kitchen door bursts open and in hobbles a very pissed off Archie. Unable to get out, Hannah finds herself trapped with Archie moving menacingly towards her.

                    ARCHIE
          Trying to escape are we!

Hannah quickly looks about her for anything she can use to defend herself but the only things in easy reach are two cooking pots and a potato knife. She picks up one of the pots and hurls it at Archie.

                    HANNAH
          Get away from me!

Hannah picks up the remaining pot and throws it. As Archie plays with her, inching himself menacingly closer, she picks up the potato knife and holds it in a threatening posture. He laughs and pulls out a large hunting knife.

INT. CAL'S CAR. DARTMOOR. DAY. (1966)

In a rural area, Cal has pulled the car over and is studying a road map that is spread across the front passenger seat. As he does, a troop of Royal Marines, on exercise, run past the car in full battle kit.

On the move again he sees a signpost that indicates 'Widecombe in the moor'. He then turns into a narrow country road - the wintry landscape looking more bleak and remote with every mile.

INT. LAND ROVER. DARTMOOR. DAY. (1966)

Bob and Bruce are driving along a single-track road.

> BOBBY
> You sure you know your way
> about this place?

> BRUCE
> I ran escape and evasion
> exercises out here in the
> Marines. I know it like the
> back of my hand.

A thought enters Bruce's head, distracting him momentarily.

> BRUCE (Cont'd)
> Shit. I left my wallet.

INT. BEDROOM. COTTAGE. DARTMOOR. DAY. (1966)

The first thing we see is Archie's reflection in a wall mirror examining a fairly deep cut on his cheek.

> ARCHIE
> You're going to pay for this!

Archie then turns round towards a bed where we see Hannah, again, lying tied and gagged. Archie, with large hunting knife in hand, moves on to the bed and straddles her. He then starts to rub his hands up and down her thighs.

> ARCHIE (Cont'd)
> What's the matter, don't
> fancy me? You think you're
> far too special for the likes
> of me don't you?

Holding his knife against her face, Archie runs his hands up her body, under her jumper and on to her breasts.

> ARCHIE (Cont'd)
> Well, you're not so special
> now are you.

Bruce suddenly walks in taking Archie by surprise.

                    BRUCE
          ARCHIE!!

                    ARCHIE
          Bruce. You were quick?

Bruce launches himself at Archie, grabs the hand holding the knife forcing him to drop it. He then grabs Archie and flings him head first out of the room into the hallway, where he crash lands in an undignified heap. As Bobby quickly moves to unbind a very relieved Hannah, an angry looking Bruce picks up the knife and confronts Archie.

                    BRUCE
          What the fuck do you think
          you're playing at!?

                    ARCHIE
          What's the problem!?

Bruce reaches down to Archie, who is lying on the floor, grabs him forcefully around the neck, lifts him up and pins him hard up against the wall.

                    BRUCE
You're the fucking problem!

                    ARCHIE
She tried to escape!
Look, the bitch cut me!

                    HANNAH
That isn't true. He attacked
me. I was only defending
myself!

                    ARCHIE
That's crap, I never touched
her... on Mum's life!
        (Beat)
What are you looking at me
like that for? Who do you
believe. Me, or that snotty
bitch!?

In a sudden move that surprises everyone,
Bruce punches Archie very hard in the
stomach, doubling him up and causing him to
slither down to the floor.

> BRUCE
> (Holding knife)
> You go near her again, or do
> anything else to fuck up this
> mission, I swear, brother or
> no brother, I'll ram this so
> far up your arse they'll hear
> you in Timbuk-fucking-tu!...
> Understand!?
> (Beat)
> Now get off your arse and
> start loading the Land
> Rover...

EXT. RURAL AREA. DARTMOOR. DAY. (1966)

On a single track road, in a very remote part
of Dartmoor, Cal's filthy Jaguar pulls up and
stops. Inside the car he studies an O.S. map.
He looks out towards a large mist shrouded
hill in the distance. (Approx 2 miles away)

He then turns and drives onto a rough unmade
track that heads in the direction of the
large hill. Within a few yards the car
grounds causing the rear wheels to spin.
Frustrated, he switches off the engine. (Ad-
lib, etc.)

As Cal gets out the car he immediately feels the biting chill. He quickly reaches behind the front seats and yanks out a thick woollen polo neck sweater and puts it on - followed by waterproof cagoule/Jacket, gloves and a woolly hat.

He then reaches into the front glove compartment, takes out the pistol that Ollie gave him and puts it in a zipped side pocket.

Cal then walks round to the boot of the car, opens it and removes the holdall. He then trudges off towards the large hill - as it begins to rain/sleet.

LATER. FURTHER UPHILL.

Making his way up the hill, the going becomes steeper and tougher. Although there is a track to follow the heavy rain is making it wet and slippery. A small loose boulder gives way and Cal slithers down a few feet. He curses, gets back on his feet and carries on.

HILL SUMMIT.

Cal finally reaches the top of the hill. He stops to catch his breath for a few moments before scanning the wet and blustery peak for any sign of the Gemmells. He looks at his watch then starts to walk - looking and shouting in all directions.

> CAL
> GEMMELL!!... GEMMELL!!...

There is no response. Cal begins to look very agitated. From behind him we hear the sound of a pistol being cocked. Cal freezes then slowly turns.

> BRUCE
> The Calvin Rennie I knew
> and despised would have
> died at the sight of his
> first blister.

Cal is confronted by Bruce, who is pointing a pistol at him. (Bruce is wearing a thick jacket and layers of clothing under overalls)

                    BRUCE (Cont'd)
          But I suppose that's all
          part of your miraculous
          transformation.

                    CAL
          Where's Hannah!?

                    BRUCE
          Where's the money?

Callum throws the holdall down on the
ground.

                    CAL
          Twenty five grand in used
          notes. Now where is she?

                    BRUCE
          She's safe.

                    CAL
          I want to see her, now!

                    BRUCE
          First things first.

Bruce walks towards the Holdall, keeping his pistol trained on Cal. When he reaches the holdall he bends down and unzips it. It contains bundles of bank notes.

> CAL
>
> I promise you Gemmell if you've done anything to her, so help me God I'll...

> BRUCE
>
> You'll what!?...

> CAL
>
> I've honoured my side of the bargain, now you honour yours!

> BRUCE
>
> Now correct me if I'm wrong but I clearly remember instructing you not to tell anyone, or contact the police.

> CAL
>
> Yeah?

Bruce removes a pair of binoculars from around his neck and hands them to Cal. He then points down from the hilltops panoramic view, in the direction of a parked police car.

                    BRUCE
        Explain 'Z' cars then?

Cal looks through the binoculars. From lens POV we see CU of the parked police car.

                    CAL
        Shit... Ollie... This has
        nothing to do with me, I
        swear it...
        The only other person who
        knows is Ollie!

                    BRUCE
        You must think I'm fucking
        simple.

                    CAL
        For the love of Christ man!
        On my life! I don't want them
        involved anymore than you do!

                    BRUCE
        On your knees!

                    CAL
        What?

Bruce suddenly lunges forward at Cal, puts
his free arm around his neck and stomps his
foot down onto Callum's calf, just below
the knee, causing him to collapse down onto
his knees.

                   BRUCE
        I SAID ON YOUR FUCKING KNEES
        NOW!!
                (Pointing gun)
        Now stay and don't move!

Bruce then starts to remove random stacks
of cash from the holdall, flicking through
each pile to check authenticity and value.
As he does this he is still holding his
pistol but no longer pointing it.

                    CAL
        That cop car could be there
        for any number of reasons...
        If you do anything to Hannah
        or me, the police will hunt
        you down. Not just here but
        all over the world.

Slowly, Cal starts to slide a hand over towards his cagoule side pocket — the pocket containing the small pistol.

                    CAL (Cont'd)
          You'll never get the chance
          to spend one penny of that
          money.

Cal's hand reaches the pocket & gingerly takes hold of the pistol. As Bruce is preoccupied, Cal bides his time for a suitable opportunity. His heartbeat is thumping hard, it is now or never. Seconds later, with a surge of courage, he pulls out the pistol and quickly jumps to his feet.

                    CAL (Cont'd)
          DROP THE GUN — NOW!!

                    BRUCE
          You've got to be fucking
          kidding me.

                    CAL
          I MEAN IT GEMMELL.
          DROP THE GUN OR I'LL DROP
          YOU!!

Bruce calmly puts his pistol down on the ground.

CAL (Cont'd)
NOW BACK AWAY... DO IT!

Bruce backs away. Cal then moves closer to Bruce, pointing the pistol at his groin.

CAL (Cont'd)
Now take me to Hannah or say
bye, bye to your balls!

BRUCE
You don't know much about
guns do you?

CAL
Enough to shoot you.

BRUCE
That's a two two pistol. From
where you're standing it
hasn't the clout to penetrate
a lump of cheese let alone
all the gear I've got on.

CAL
Thanks for the tip. I'll move
a bit closer then.

Cal moves in very close to Bruce (To within four feet) kicking Bruce's pistol out of reach as he does.

CAL (Cont'd)
Now for the last time.
Where is Hannah!?

BRUCE
Fuck you pop star.

Cal, almost at the end of his tether, loses his cool and moves aggressively forward with the intention of sticking the barrel of the pistol right in Bruce's face.

CAL
WHAT HAVE YOU DONE WITH HER!!

Unfortunately for Cal, his emotions play right into Bruce's hands. As he moves to within an arm's length, Bruce instantly leaps forward and with split second timing grabs the pistol, twists it from Cal's grip and strikes him hard in the face causing him to crumple to the ground.

                    BRUCE
          You ungrateful little SHIT!
          ... I SAVE YOU THOUSANDS AND
          YOU THREATEN TO SHOOT MY
          BALLS OFF!!

As Cal lies stunned on the wet ground,
hands over his face with blood streaming
out of his nose, Bruce picks up his own gun
and wipes the dirt off it.

                    CAL
          What are you on about?

Bruce moves close to Cal and bends down on
one knee.

                    BRUCE
          Andrew bloody Wishart!...
          He was blackmailing you
          wasn't he?

                    CAL
          But how did?...

                    BRUCE
          Because he was a greedy cunt
          who found out who you really
          are.

                    CAL
              (After beat)
         It was you... You killed him?

Bruce doesn't deny it but his expression
says it all.

                    CAL (Cont'd)
         Oh Jesus...

                    BRUCE
         Don't you 'Oh Jesus' me -
         as if you give a shit.

                    CAL
         There was no need to blow
         his fucking brains out!

                    BRUCE
         There was every need!... One
         less parasitical old poof to
         blab his mouth off, and one
         very relieved pop star with
         a shit load of cash going
         spare.

LATER.

Cal is kneeling on the ground in an 'execution' style position with hands placed on top of his head. Bruce is standing right behind with his pistol pointing at the back of Cal's head.

From this point on we only see a close up of Cal. He is soaking wet, shivering and a mixture of dirt, blood & water is running out of his nose and down his face.

> CAL
> Look what ever happened
> between you and me, stays
> with you and me, alright...
> I'm not like Wishart, I've
> got just as much to lose as
> you do. If not more!

Cal now begins to look very anxious. Bruce says nothing.

>   CAL (Cont'd)
> For God's sake, you've got
> what you wanted, there's no
> need for this... All I want
> is Hannah!...
>   (Beat)
> You know what Gemmell, fuck
> it!... Do with me what you
> like... But please don't hurt
> her — she's got nothing to
> do with this and you fucking
> know it!!

Bruce remains silent. Cal then closes his eyes and braces himself for the shot that will end his life. A few agonising moments later Bruce steps from behind. Cal opens his eyes and finds Bruce standing in front of him.

                    BRUCE
I was watching one of these
'unexplained mysteries' shows
on TV the other night. You
know, spooks, aliens and all
that shite. But to my great
frustration they failed to
mention the biggest, most
baffling mystery of them all…
          (Beat)
How the fuck a pathetic little
shit like you, returns from
the dead and transforms himself
from sugar plum fairy into
the pop sensation that is
Jack Dallas?... Now to me that
really is a fucking mystery.

                    CAL
          (After beat)
You really want to know?

                    BRUCE
I really do.

                    CAL
Calvin Rennie never returned
from the dead... But Jack
Dallas did.

Bruce is stumped by Cal's spooky enigmatic answer. He's not sure if Cal is being serious or not and thinks on it momentarily. (As daft as it sounds it kind of makes sense)

> BRUCE
> Go back and head north. In six miles there's a white cottage set back off the road. Your girlfriend's there... But I'd hurry if I were you...

Bruce then casually walks away. As he does, Cal ponders the situation. Having resigned himself to being killed, Bruce's sudden change of heart is a big relief. Moments later Cal cautiously looks behind him and Bruce is nowhere to be seen.

We then see Cal charging, falling and sliding down the wet hill as fast as he can.

EXT. OTHERSIDE OF HILL. DARTMOOR. DAY. (1966)

On the opposite downward slope of the large hill (or similar interesting terrain) we see Bruce running down as fast as he can, carrying the holdall full of cash.

We then see the Gemmell's Land Rover parked in a valley with camouflage netting over it. Waiting nervously by it are Bob & Archie, both fully kitted out in Royal Marine combat fatigues — plus rifles, Green Berets and camouflaged painted faces.

The second they spot their brother running towards them, both spring into action and start removing the camouflage netting, revealing military index plates and insignia, etc.

Bruce makes straight for the rear of the Land Rover, opens the door, and puts the holdall inside. He then quickly removes his donkey jacket and overalls — revealing Marine combat fatigues underneath.

ARCHIE
Well — did you get it?

                    BRUCE
Yeah!... But I think the cops
might be in on it.

                    BOBBY
Shit..

                    ARCHIE
I thought you said Rennie
wouldn't dare!?

                    BRUCE
I don't think he did.

                    BOBBY
Then who?

                    BRUCE
Most likely his manager.

                    ARCHIE
So he blabbed... Did you kill
him?

                    BRUCE
No.

                    ARCHIE
NO?!

                    BRUCE
        It serves no purpose.

                    ARCHIE
        He knows who we are! What
        better reason is there!?

                    BRUCE
        If we go down so does he.
        Rennie won't risk it. He's
        got far too much to lose.

                    ARCHIE
        How the fuck do you know!

Annoyed, Bruce grabs Archie tightly by the
collar.

                    BRUCE
        Are you going to be a stupid
        cunt all your life! This way
        we might just get away with
        it. So stop complaining,
        stick to the plan and do what
        I fucking told you.

Archie says nothing but we can see that he
is less than pleased at being put in his
place once again.

EXT. RURAL AREA. DARTMOOR. DAY. (1966)

Exhausted and bedraggled, Callum reaches his car. He gets in, starts the engine and slams it into reverse. The rear wheels spin as the tyres scramble for traction on the wet track. To his great relief they finally grip enabling him to reverse back down the track.

EXT. REMOTE TERRAIN. DARTMOOR. DAY. (1966)

With Bruce at the wheel, the Gemmell's Land Rover crashes, bumps and splashes, over rough terrain and unmade tracks.

Miles away but in similar terrain, we see the green Land Rover descending a rough piece of land and onto a single track tarmac road.

EXT. RURAL ROAD. DARTMOOR. DAY. (1966)

With daylight beginning to fade, Callum is thrashing along a narrow tarmac road. As he drives we see he is desperately looking for signs of the 'white cottage'.

A bit further on he spots a white cottage nestled in a small valley. He slams on the brakes and searches for a road in. He looks behind and notices a small track that might lead to the house. Once again Cal crunches the gear stick into reverse and blazes backwards.

We then see Cal's mud splattered E-type hammering rally style along a single track that leads to the cottage. The track is so unsuitable that part of the exhaust pipe is torn off as it crashes along.

EXT. 'A' ROAD EAST. DARTMOOR. DAY. (1966)

On a major 'A' road out of Dartmoor, the police have set up a road block and are checking every vehicle, causing a tailback of several cars. We then see the Gemmell's Land Rover stationary at the side of the road, hidden behind trees approx a quarter of a mile away.

INT. LAND ROVER. A ROAD. DARTMOOR. DAY. (1966)

Bruce is looking through his binoculars at the road block ahead. Bob and Archie are looking pretty worried.

> BOB
> They're stopping and
> searching everyone.

From down the road a small convoy of Royal Marine vehicles, consisting of two Land Rovers and two three tonne trucks appear.

> BRUCE
> Not everyone.

As the last truck rolls past, the Gemmell's Land Rover pulls out from behind the trees and tags onto the end of the convoy. As the convoy approaches the police road block it is immediately waved through... And the Gemmell's with it.

As they pass Bruce gives the policemen a small courteous wave. They respond in kind.

EXT. WHITE COTTAGE. DARTMOOR. DAY. (1966)

The battered E-type slams to a halt outside the cottage. Cal scrambles out of the car and runs to the house shouting Hannah's name.

He looks desperately in one of the windows but all he can see in the darkness is the faint glow of a dying fire. He shouts Hannah again but she doesn't answer. He then runs to the front door and pushes it open.

The first thing Cal notices is the sound of running water. As he steps forward, his boots splash into water two inches deep. Suddenly the ransom photo of Hannah, tied up in the bath, flashes through his mind.

                    CAL
          Oh dear Jesus no!...
          HANNAH!

Callum splashes through the flooded hallway to a door where water is gushing out from underneath. He immediately grabs the door handle and pushes, only to find it locked. From within he can hear the distinct sound of water pouring into an over running bath.

Now panicked, Cal tries to force the door. Then, summoning every ounce of strength, he steps back and rams the door with his shoulder. The door bursts open illuminating the flooded bathroom and the overflowing bath tub. Fearing the worst he looks into the bath.

To his immense relief Hannah isn't in it. He turns off the tap and walks back out into the hallway, calling her name. Just as he is about to enter another room, he hears (above his splashing footsteps) a faint mumbling coming from behind a closed cupboard door.

Cal quickly opens the door where to his absolute joy he finds Hannah gagged and tied but otherwise unharmed.

The second Hannah is free the pair embrace with profound emotion.

EXT/INT. LAND ROVER. A ROAD. DAY. (1966)

With daylight fading, the Gemmell's Land Rover is still following the Marine convoy on an 'A' road heading east towards Exeter. They pass a police car and motorcycle parked up in a lay-by. A bit further on two police vans, with blue lights flashing, pass by heading in the opposite direction.

We see the Land Rover break off and turn down a narrow road.

                    BOBBY
          How much further?

                    BRUCE
          About five miles.

EXT. REMOTE AREA. BY RIVER. NIGHT. (1966)

The Gemmell's Land Rover is steadily making its way over a rough unmade track. In the headlight beam they come to a closed wooden gate. Archie jumps out and opens it. After the Land Rover is driven through, Archie shuts the gate and gets back in the front passenger side.

The land Rover carries on a short distance until it reaches a flat timber bridge spanning a narrow river. The bridge is only wide enough to accommodate tractors and small agricultural vehicles.

Bruce carefully drives over the bridge which has no barriers marking the edge of each side. Once over the river, the Land Rover is driven a short distance then halts next to a short wooden jetty.

BRUCE
(To Archie)
You know what to do.

Archie nods. Bruce and Bobby exit the Land Rover then walk along the jetty to where a small military type inflatable boat is tied up.

                    BRUCE (Cont'd)
            Bob - bring the gear.

Meanwhile Archie has walked to the back of
the Land Rover and opened the rear door.
Stowed to the side is a fuel Jerrycan.
Archie lifts out the can which is full of
fuel. As he does his attention is drawn to
the holdall containing the ransom money.

Archie looks in the direction of his brothers
and then at the holdall. We can see what
is going through his mind. Moments later
Bobby runs up and begins removing gear and
weapons from the vehicle.

                    BOBBY
            Bruce said make sure you
            give the front seats a
            real good soaking.

                    ARCHIE
            Do you think I'm fucking
            simple or something.

Bobby grabs hold of the holdall containing the ransom cash and puts it down on the ground. He then slings a rucksack over one shoulder and two rifles over the other. With his remaining free hand he then makes to pick up the holdall.

                    ARCHIE (Cont'd)
          Don't worry about that, I'll
          bring it with the rest of the
          gear.

                    BOBBY
          It's okay, I've got it.

As Bob goes to walk away carrying the holdall, Archie is infused with frustration. It is now or never. He picks up an iron wheel brace lying on the cargo floor.

                    ARCHIE
          Bob...

As Bobby turns to see what his brother wants, Archie strikes him hard around the side of the head, knocking him cold.

Archie quickly picks up the holdall, slings it in the back of the Land Rover and runs to the driver's door.

Bruce is walking along the jetty towards the Land Rover when its engine and lights turn on. Then, just as he notices Bobby's unconscious body slumped on the ground, the Land Rover accelerates away leaving him stunned.

Bruce is quick to realise what is happening. He screams Archie's name and tries his determined best to give chase. Running at the accelerating vehicle, he withdraws his pistol and fires several shots at it.

When Bruce reaches Bob he is relieved to find him semi conscious but badly dazed. He immediately picks up one of the LA1A rifles that Bobby was carrying, cocks it and fires a dozen or so well aimed shots at the Land Rover.

Driving as fast as possible in the semi darkness, Archie makes it to the wooden bridge spanning the river.

Just as the Land Rover manoeuvres onto the bridge, a bullet slams into one of the front tyres, deflating it instantly causing sudden loss of control. The front wheel slips off the bridge and the 4X4 rolls off, landing upside down in the cold dark water.

The river is swollen and fast flowing. Although not quite deep enough to completely submerge the vehicle, the Land Rover immediately begins to sink nose first. Upside down, with seconds to escape, Archie gasps as the freezing water pours into the pitch-black cabin.

He manages to open the driver's door but as he tries to manoeuvre himself out, he finds one of his boots trapped between the clutch and brake pedal. With the water rising rapidly, he tries desperately to free his foot but the more frantically he pulls the more stuck it becomes.

As the car sinks further Archie begins to panic. He contorts his body in last-ditch effort to keep his head above water. Seconds later he is forced to hold his breath. Every moment that passes intensifies his feelings of disorientation and panic as his oxygen-starved lungs scream for air.

Bruce sprints to the bridge and immediately begins to remove his boots and clothes.

Within 30 seconds the Land Rover has almost totally submerged. All that is visible above the moonlit water are the rear wheels, bumper and the bottom half of the rear door. As soon as Bruce has stripped to his Y-fronts he dives straight in. (clenching small rubber torch between teeth)

Bruce is underwater for well over two minutes. He then surfaces, gasping & replenishing his lungs. He then swims the short distance to the bank with an object under one arm. The cash holdall.

Bruce then turns about and dives back under again.

UNDER WATER

Bruce's torch illuminates Archie's face. His eyes are staring wide open and his motionless expression is frozen in terror.

SERIES OF SHOTS D.

D1. NEWSPAPER HEADLINE.

Headline reads: *DARTMOOR PRISON ESCAPE. ALL FIVE RECAPTURED.*

D2. CAL & HANNAH'S HOUSE.

All of the band members, Ollie, and the girlfriends are gathered. Moments later Cal and Hannah enter the room. Both are welcomed home with hugs and kisses.

D3. DEVON. SOUTH COAST.

The body of Archie Gemmell floats down the mouth of a Devonshire river and is washed out into the English Channel.

D4. TV STUDIO (1967).

The Barracuda's are live on TV belting out their latest single.

D5. MELODY MAKER.

Close up of singles chart. Latest single is at number one.

D6. ALBUM COVER.

We see a close up of the album cover 'Fishy business'- The Barracuda's second LP. Again the cover is simply a cool shot of the band in a cool London location.

D7. MELODY MAKER.

A close up of the 'Melody Maker' Album chart, of May 1967, shows The Barracuda's at No 1 with 'Fishy Business'. The Monkees are at No 2 with 'More of the Monkees' & The Sound of Music is at No 3.

EXT. SOUTHEND PIER. ENGLAND. NIGHT. (1967)

At the pier head, we see an unsteady, dishevelled and troubled looking Krys Winslow, swig back the last couple of mouthfuls from a bottle of whiskey.

After throwing the bottle over the side, he climbs over the guard rail (A sign on rail warns: *DANGER DEEP WATER*) and with no hesitation, lets go of the rail and allows himself to fall head first.

INT/EXT. RESTAURANT. LONDON. NIGHT. (1967)

In the reception area of an upmarket restaurant, we see the smartly dressed foursome of Cal, Hannah, Ollie and Jana, as they are about to leave. The Maitre d' bids them a fond farewell and the smiling (Afro-Caribbean) doorman, IRVINE, opens the doors. (Ad-lib dialogue etc. Hannah is wearing a white silk scarf)

After Ollie's Rolls Royce pulls up outside the restaurant, the foursome are escorted to the car under the cover of Irvine's huge umbrella. (It is raining)

We then become aware of a man standing in a recessed shop doorway a few yards away. He is dressed in a dark trench coat, a scarf covers his lower face and a Fedora hat casts a shadow over his eyes.

As the chauffeur opens the limo rear door, Jana, followed by Ollie and Hannah get in. Just as Cal is about to ingress he turns to Irvine, holding out a five pound note.

Suddenly the man in the trench coat barges past Irvine, pulling out a small revolver from his coat pocket. At point blank range he fires five rounds at Cal - hitting him in several places. As Cal slithers down onto the rain lashed street the assassin flees.

Ollie immediately leaps out of the car and runs round to where Cal is slumped on the pavement. Whilst he does, Irving bravely runs after the gunman.

> OLLIE
> OH MY GOD!... Oh my god!!
> JACK! can you hear me!?...
> Jack!? JACK?!!

Cal manages to groan an expletive. His eyes are only partially open and a trickle of blood is coming out of his nose and mouth.

Ollie takes the clean white handkerchief from his top jacket pocket and uses it to stem the blood from the wound that is bleeding most. (Ad-lib dialogue, etc)

> OLLIE (Cont'd)
> SOMEBODY CALL AN AMBULANCE
> NOW!!

Ollie's Chauffeur dashes into the restaurant to call for help. As he does we become aware of Rosie watching in the background.

> OLLIE (Cont'd)
> Hannah, quick, your scarf..
> HANNAH!

Ollie then looks into the rear of the limo. To his horror he finds Hannah slumped on the back seat with blood streaming from a neck wound (due to the chaos no one has noticed)

EXT. STREET. LONDON. NIGHT. (1967)

Meanwhile a hundred yards or so up the street, Irving is catching up on the assassin who is beginning to flag. The gunman stops and fires off a panicked and badly aimed shot — forcing the doorman to take cover.

Just as the assassin turns to continue his escape, he steps off the pavement and runs slap bang into the side of a taxi. Knocked cold, he slithers to the ground, his hat falls off and he drops the gun.

First thing Irvine does is kick away the gun. He then bends down, turns the unconscious assassin onto his back and pulls the scarf down from around his face — revealing it to be Krys Winslow.

RESUME CAL/LIMO.

Sirens, blue lights and commotion. Cal's life blood ebbs from his body and blends with the rain soaked pavement (His hand still holding the five pound note)

Moments later his fingers relax, the note falls to the ground and is blown into the gutter where it is carried along by a small stream of crimson coloured rainwater.

Photographic flash. Fade to intense brilliant white light.

INT. HOSPITAL. LONDON. DAY. (1967)

Callum is lying unconscious in an intensive
care ward, hooked up to a drip and wearing an
oxygen mask with a Cardiograph registering a
very weak pulse. A NURSE (2) is in attendance.

WARD WAITING AREA.

Outside the ward, the rest of the band are
seated in the waiting area — each looking
haggard, red eyed and shell-shocked. Ollie,
still in his blood stained suit, is talking
to a SURGEON.

>   SURGEON
>   Frankly I don't know what's
>   keeping him alive. The next
>   few hours will be critical.

INTENSIVE CARE WARD.

Resume Cal in Bed. Rosie has now appeared.

>   ROSIE
>   Cal, what is going on?

We then become aware of Cal's spiritual
form standing in the corner of the room.

                    CAL
What took you so long?

                   ROSIE
What do you think you're
playing at?

                    CAL
Amazing eh. Punctured lung,
half a kidney shot away and
a ruptured femoral artery… I
lost four and a half pints of
blood.

                   ROSIE
You should be dead.

                    CAL
I'm not though... Gemmell
must be getting sloppy.

                   ROSIE
Gemmell?.. It wasn't Gemmell.
He's in Barbados.

                    CAL
Really. Who the fuck
was it then?

                    ROSIE

Krys Winslow.

                    CAL

KRYS WINSLOW!?... I thought
he jumped off Southend Pier?

                    ROSIE

He did... But like everything
else he managed to fuck it up.

                    CAL

How do you jump off Southend
Pier and fuck it up!?

                    ROSIE

The tide was out... Talk
about top of the plops.

                    CAL

Fucking bastard! What did
I ever do to him?

                    ROSIE

Well apart taking over his
band, drugging him, beating
him up and stealing his
girlfriend, your guess is
as good as mine.

                    CAL
Don't give me that, he never
liked me from the start...
He was always jealous of my
songs.

                    ROSIE
Your songs!?

                    CAL
You know what I mean.

                    ROSIE
Anyway, you've had your fun,
the adventure's over. It's
time to go back.

                    CAL
        (After beat)
And what if I don't want to
go back?

                    ROSIE
What do you mean, what if
you don't want to?
Everything's been sorted.

                    CAL
So how come I'm still here then?

ROSIE

You're fighting it. It's
time to let go.

CAL

Maybe I don't want to.

ROSIE

What?

CAL

Sorry Rosie but I'm not going
anywhere. I'm staying right
here with Hannah and everyone
else.

ROSIE

Look I know you love Hannah
and being a pop star and all
the good stuff that goes with
it, but let's not get too
carried away here.

CAL

It's a bit late for all that.

                    ROSIE

Aw, Jesus, I knew this would
happen. Why did I let you
play in that bloody pub!

                    CAL

You know why...

                    ROSIE

Cal, reality check. This is
a parallel universe. You have
to return to your own and to
your own life!

                    CAL

Oh wow, I can't wait to get
back to that. Playing in pubs
for pennies, a string of
failed relationships, a job
that makes every hour feel
like a month... Return to
my life, it might as well
be as a fucking cabbage!

                    ROSIE

But things can change. It
doesn't have to be like that.

                    CAL
    Yeah too right it doesn't.
    Here I'm living the dream
    not just dreaming it. I feel
    alive, life is interesting,
    it means something, I mean
    something!

                   ROSIE
              (After beat)
    Okay, if that's the way you
    want it... But understand
    this. If you choose to remain
    there's no going back, not
    ever... and you know what
    that means.

                    CAL
              (After pause for thought)
    I can't leave, I can't
    leave Hannah.

Rosie sighs a deep reluctant sigh.

                    ROSIE
          I was hoping it wouldn't
          come to this...
          There's something you
          should know...
                (Beat)
          Hannah's gone.

                    CAL
          Gone... Gone where?

                    ROSIE
          She caught one of the bullets
          that was meant for you...
          She died in the ambulance...
          I am so sorry...

Cal is absolutely devastated. As he processes
the news his feelings of profound sadness
are communicated without dialogue.

As this happens his spiritual form becomes
increasingly more solid until it reaches
100%. A close up of the cardiograph attached
to his unconscious body, registers a couple
of weakening pulses then flat lines. Fade to
white.

NEWSPAPER FRONT PAGE. (PRESENT DAY)

Close up of the front page of the Glasgow Herald. It says: *'ICE RESCUE HERO SET TO MAKE FULL RECOVERY'*. Underneath is a photo of Callum taken in hospital.

INT. HOSPITAL. GLASGOW. NIGHT.

Cal, with his frost bitten hands and feet bandaged, is sitting up in bed chatting with his MOTHER, Brother SCOTT, close friends and family. His bed side area/cabinets, etc, are covered in cards and gifts from well wishers.

INT. LARGE PUB. GLASGOW. NIGHT.

Cal, accompanied by Sean and brother SCOTT, enters the saloon bar of the 'Celtic Heart' where a group of friends welcome him back with a loud cheer, handshakes and kisses from the girls.

LATER.

We then enter a semi-surreal scene as Cal mentally steps back from the conversation and laughter around him. The first thing that takes his notice is a news program on the television above the bar. The news reporter is doing a live broadcast from a street in Manchester.

The reporter is OLIVER JACKMAN (Same actor as Ollie Jackson)

>   OLIVER JACKMAN (On TV)
>   Leaving the people of this
>   city asking - 'Just how
>   long will it be before the
>   spectre of gun culture casts
>   its shadow over yet another
>   innocent young victim?'...
>   Oliver Jackman... BBC news,
>   Manchester.

Standing by the bar are three hard looking men. One of them is BRUCE DALLAS. (Same actor who plays Bruce Gemmell) and he is talking to big Tam.

> BRUCE
>
> If that wee cunt doesn't tell me what I need to know, I'll come over and wipe the fucking smile of his face!…

The big stocky man acknowledges and leaves immediately. Bruce then turns to a barman who has his head buried in a copy of 'The Stage' a theatrical newspaper.

> BRUCE (Cont'd)
>
> Hey — Ben Affleck!

The barman instantly puts down the paper revealing the him to be Bobby Gemmell. (Same age as in 1960's)

> BOBBY
>
> Sorry Bruce — same again?

                    BRUCE
        Aye, and one for yourself.
              (Mobile rings. He answers)
        Detective Inspector Dallas.

Moments later Cal is approached by REV
MACANDREW (Same actor who plays Andrew
Wishart)

                REV MACANDREW
        Callum!

                    CAL
        Reverend MacAndrew.

                REV MACANDREW
        How the devil are you my Boy?

As Callum and the Rev chat we pull out to
see Rosie watching unseen in the background.
She smiles to herself.

INT. CALLUM'S PARENTS HOUSE. DAY.

Cal is sitting in the living room of his
mother's house. His Grandmother, GRANDMA,
hands him an old family photo album.

> GRANDMA
> I came across this. I want
> you to have it.

Intrigued, Cal takes the album and turns
over the hardback leather cover. We then
cut to a couple of close ups of sepia tone
family photographs mounted in the book.

> CAL
> This is great.
> Thanks Grandma.

Another picture is a black and white photo
of a wedding couple in their early twenties.
The groom is a tall well built man dressed
in a Royal Marine uniform.

Underneath it is the picture of the young man with the Elvis style haircut sitting astride a powerful motorcycle with a younger man standing beside. Written under it is *DAD, BILLY & CALVIN 1955*. (Same picture as on Callums's fireplace)

As Cal turns the next page he is presented with an astounding image that sends a shiver running down his spine. The photo is a colour shot of Calvin Rennie, posing next to a street sign saying *'CARNABY STREET'*. The same photograph he saw on the mantel in Calvin Rennie's tenement. However, this copy has been badly singed by fire. Callum is aghast.

                    CAL
          Who's this guy?

                    GRANDMA
          My brother Calvin.

                    CAL'S MUM
          I've never seen a photo of
          him at that age before.

> GRANDMA
>
> My father burned all of
> his photos. My mother managed
> to rescued a few but this
> is the only one taken of
> him before... You know...

> CAL'S MUM
>
> It's a crying shame —
> so it is.

> GRANDMA
>
> Aye, things were a lot
> different back then.

We leave the scene with Cal pondering his startling discovery. He isn't quite sure what to make of it but after a few moments contemplating the irony he smiles contentedly to himself.

EXT. MUSIC SHOP. GLASGOW. DAY.

Cal, with friends and family (including the young boy he saved and his parents) are standing on the pavement outside a newly fitted shop, watching a tradesman fitting the last letter to a sign above. The name *BARRACUDA MUSIC* is revealed. Rosie is watching.

> ROSIE (V.O.)
> They say that you never know what surprises lie around life's corners...
> > (Beat)
> It turned out that the father of the young boy Cal pulled from the frozen lake was a multi-millionaire businessman with a great passion for music.

INT. MUSIC SHOP. GLASGOW. DAY.

Inside, Barracuda Music is a well stocked
Aladdin's cave full of amps, speakers,
guitars, percussion and keyboards, etc. The
shop is busy and we see Cal giving a customer
a wicked demonstration on an electric guitar.

> ROSIE (V.O. Cont'd)
> So grateful was he for the
> life of his son that he
> bankrolled a new business and
> as a reward gave Callum a
> fifty percent partnership.
> (Beat)
> And although Cal knows he'll
> never be a pop star, I can
> honestly say for the first time
> in his life, I've never seen
> him happier... Well, almost...

Callum is in the shop when a very attractive
twenty something year old woman, EMMA walks
in. She approaches him.

                    EMMA
                (Scots)
        Excuse me. I am looking for
        Callum Rennie, the manager?

When Cal looks up at her his eyes pop
and his jaw drops. Emma is the spitting
image of Hannah Jensen. (Played by same
actress.)

                    CAL
        That's me.

                    EMMA
        Hi... My name's Emma Wilson.
        I was told you were looking
        for a part time sales
        assistant?

                    CAL
        But we haven't even
        advertised yet. Who told you?

                    EMMA
        A friend of yours.
                (Beat)
        She said her name was
        Rosie... Rosie Marsh —
        from London.

                    CAL
          When can you start?

Delighted reaction from Emma, ad-lib, etc.

Cal can hardly believe it. Moments later
he looks up towards the ceiling and smiles
knowingly.

FADE OUT

                  THE END

Printed in Great Britain
by Amazon